W9-AEE-324

Children, Violence, and Murder

CRIME, JUSTICE, AND PUNISHMENT

Children, Violence, and Murder

Richard Worth

Austin Sarat, GENERAL EDITOR

CHELSEA HOUSE PUBLISHERS
Philadelphia

Chelsea House Publishers

Editor in Chief Sally Cheney
Production Manager Pamela Loos
Art Director Sara Davis
Director of Photography Judy L. Hasday
Managing Editor James D. Gallagher
Senior Production Editor J. Christopher Higgins

**Staff for CHILDREN, VIOLENCE,
AND MURDER**

Senior Editor John Ziff
Associate Art Director Takeshi Takahashi
Picture Researcher Patricia Burns
Designer Emiliano Begnardi/Takeshi Takahashi
Cover Illustrator Mary Brady

© 2001 by Chelsea House Publishers, a subsidiary of
Haights Cross Communications. All rights reserved.
Printed and bound in the United States of America.

First Printing

1 3 5 7 9 8 6 4 2

The Chelsea House World Wide Web address is
http://www.chelseahouse.com

Library of Congress Cataloging-in-Publication Data

Worth, Richard.
Children, violence, and murder / Richard Worth.
  p. cm. — (Crime, justice, and punishment)
Includes bibliographical references and index.

ISBN 0-7910-5154-4

1. Children and violence—Juvenile literature. [1. Violence.
2. Murder.] I. Title. II. Series.

HQ784.V55 W67 2000
303.6'083—dc21
                          00-031650

Contents

Fears and Fascinations:
   An Introduction to Crime,
   Justice, and Punishment
   Austin Sarat   7

1 Columbine   13

2 The Dark Side of Youth   25

3 Juvenile Violence: Individual,
         Community, and Cultural Factors   37

4   Family Violence   49

5 School Violence   59

6   Juvenile Justice   73

7 Facing the Future   87

Further Reading   92
Index   95

CRIME, JUSTICE, AND PUNISHMENT

CAPITAL PUNISHMENT

CHILDREN, VIOLENCE, AND MURDER

CLASSIC CONS AND SWINDLES

CRIMES AGAINST CHILDREN:
CHILD ABUSE AND NEGLECT

CRIMES AGAINST HUMANITY

CYBER CRIMES

DEFENSE LAWYERS

DRUGS, CRIME,
AND CRIMINAL JUSTICE

THE DUTY TO RESCUE

ESPIONAGE AND TREASON

THE FBI

THE FBI'S MOST WANTED

FORENSIC SCIENCE

GANGS AND CRIME

THE GRAND JURY

GREAT PROSECUTIONS

GREAT ROBBERIES

GUNS, CRIME, AND
THE SECOND AMENDMENT

HATE CRIMES

HIGH CRIMES AND MISDEMEANORS:
THE IMPEACHMENT PROCESS

INFAMOUS TRIALS

THE INSANITY DEFENSE

JUDGES AND SENTENCING

THE JURY SYSTEM

JUVENILE CRIME

MAJOR UNSOLVED CRIMES

ORGANIZED CRIME

PRISONS

PRIVATE INVESTIGATORS
AND BOUNTY HUNTERS

PUNISHMENT AND REHABILITATION

RACE, CRIME, AND PUNISHMENT

REVENGE AND RETRIBUTION

RIGHTS OF THE ACCUSED

SERIAL MURDER

TERRORISM

VICTIMS AND VICTIMS' RIGHTS

WHITE-COLLAR CRIME

Fears and Fascinations:

An Introduction to
Crime, Justice, and Punishment

By Austin Sarat

We live with crime and images of crime all around us. Crime evokes in most of us a deep aversion, a feeling of profound vulnerability, but it also evokes an equally deep fascination. Today, in major American cities the fear of crime is a major fact of life, some would say a disproportionate response to the realities of crime. Yet the fear of crime is real, palpable in the quickened steps and furtive glances of people walking down darkened streets. At the same time, we eagerly follow crime stories on television and in movies. We watch with a "who done it" curiosity, eager to see the illicit deed done, the investigation undertaken, the miscreant brought to justice and given his just deserts. On the streets the presence of crime is a reminder of our own vulnerability and the precariousness of our taken-for-granted rights and freedoms. On television and in the movies the crime story gives us a chance to probe our own darker motives, to ask "Is there a criminal within?" as well as to feel the collective satisfaction of seeing justice done.

Fear and fascination, these two poles of our engagement with crime, are, of course, only part of the story. Crime is, after all, a major social and legal problem, not just an issue of our individual psychology. Politicians today use our fear of, and fascination with, crime for political advantage. How we respond to crime, as well as to the political uses of the crime issue, tells us a lot about who we are as a people as well as what we value and what we tolerate. Is our response compassionate or severe? Do we seek to understand or to punish, to enact an angry vengeance or to rehabilitate and welcome the criminal back into our midst? The CRIME, JUSTICE, AND PUNISHMENT series is designed to explore these themes, to ask why we are fearful and fascinated, to probe the meanings and motivations of crimes and criminals and of our responses to them, and, finally, to ask what we can learn about ourselves and the society in which we live by examining our responses to crime.

Crime is always a challenge to the prevailing normative order and a test of the values and commitments of law-abiding people. It is sometimes a Raskolnikov-like act of defiance, an assertion of the unwillingness of some to live according to the rules of conduct laid out by organized society. In this sense, crime marks the limits of the law and reminds us of law's all-too-regular failures. Yet sometimes there is more desperation than defiance in criminal acts; sometimes they signal a deep pathology or need in the criminal. To confront crime is thus also to come face-to-face with the reality of social difference, of class privilege and extreme deprivation, of race and racism, of children neglected, abandoned, or abused whose response is to enact on others what they have experienced themselves. And occasionally crime, or what is labeled a criminal act, represents a call for justice, an appeal to a higher moral order against the inadequacies of existing law.

Figuring out the meaning of crime and the motivations of criminals and whether crime arises from defiance, desperation, or the appeal for justice is never an easy task. The motivations and meanings of crime are as varied as are the persons who engage in criminal conduct. They are as mysterious as any of the mysteries of the human soul. Yet the desire to know the secrets of crime and the criminal is a strong one, for in that knowledge may lie one step on the road to protection, if not an assurance of one's own personal safety. Nonetheless, as strong as that desire may be, there is no available technology that can allow us to know the whys of crime with much confidence, let alone a scientific certainty. We can, however, capture something about crime by studying the defiance, desperation, and quest for justice that may be associated with it. Books in the CRIME, JUSTICE, AND PUNISHMENT series will take up that challenge. They tell stories of crime and criminals, some famous, most not, some glamorous and exciting, most mundane and commonplace.

This series will, in addition, take a sober look at American criminal justice, at the procedures through which we investigate crimes and identify criminals, at the institutions in which innocence or guilt is determined. In these procedures and institutions we confront the thrill of the chase as well as the challenge of protecting the rights of those who defy our laws. It is through the efficiency and dedication of law enforcement that we might capture the criminal; it is in the rare instances of their corruption or brutality that we feel perhaps our deepest betrayal. Police, prosecutors, defense lawyers, judges, and jurors administer criminal justice and in their daily actions give substance to the guarantees of the Bill of Rights. What is an adversarial system of justice? How does it work? Why do we have it? Books in the CRIME, JUSTICE, AND PUNISHMENT series will examine the thrill of the chase as we seek to capture the criminal. They will also reveal the drama and majesty of the criminal trial as well as the day-to-day reality of a criminal justice system in which trials are the exception and negotiated pleas of guilty are the rule.

When the trial is over or the plea has been entered, when we have separated the innocent from the guilty, the moment of punishment has arrived. The injunction to punish the guilty, to respond to pain inflicted by inflicting pain, is as old as civilization itself. "An eye for an eye and a tooth for a tooth" is a biblical reminder that punishment must measure pain for pain. But our response to the criminal must be better than and different from the crime itself. The biblical admonition, along with the constitutional prohibition of "cruel and unusual punishment," signals that we seek to punish justly and to be just not only in the determination of who can and should be punished, but in how we punish as well. But neither reminder tells us what to do with the wrongdoer. Do we rape the rapist, or burn the home of the arsonist? Surely justice and decency say no. But, if not, then how can and should we punish? In a world in which punishment is neither identical to the crime nor an automatic response to it, choices must be made and we must make them. Books in the CRIME, JUSTICE, AND PUNISHMENT series will examine those choices and the practices, and politics, of punishment. How do we punish and why do we punish as we do? What can we learn about the rationality and appropriateness of today's responses to crime by examining our past and its responses? What works? Is there, and can there be, a just measure of pain?

CRIME, JUSTICE, AND PUNISHMENT brings together books on some of the great themes of human social life. The books in this series capture our fear and fascination with crime and examine our responses to it. They remind us of the deadly seriousness of these subjects. They bring together themes in law, literature, and popular culture to challenge us to think again, to think anew, about subjects that go to the heart of who we are and how we can and will live together.

*   *   *   *   *

One of the most troubling issues of our times is the sudden and visible upsurge of killing by children. The long-held image of children as carriers of an unspoiled innocence today seems wildly out-of-date.

After notorious school shootings, perhaps the most well known of which occurred at Columbine High School, it seems that children are as much the carriers of society's misplaced violent urges as are adults. Where once people could send their kids to school with little thought about their physical safety, today our schools are often heavily policed danger zones. What can be done to rescue kids from violence and to return to our children the luxury of innocence?

These issues are all addressed in *Children, Violence, and Murder*. This very readable book is filled with the best information about child violence. It reminds us of the complex sources of child violence and effectively debunks all efforts to identify any single, exclusive cause. This book tells a gripping story of the Columbine tragedy and sets up the difficult task of trying to understand and explain why children turn to violence. It effectively combines historical material with contemporary cases and explores a wide range of source material, bringing psychology, law, and family policy together. In the end, *Children, Violence, and Murder* presents a powerful argument for the need to interrupt the cycle of violence in its earliest stages and for massive social investment in the development of more nurturing environments for kids.

1.

COLUMBINE

Anguish is written on the faces of these students evacuated from Columbine High School in Littleton, Colorado, April 20, 1999.

ylan Klebold and Eric Harris, seniors at Columbine High School in the well-to-do community of Littleton, Colorado, were close friends. On April 20, 1999, the two boys arrived at school late. As Harris got out of his car, he saw another senior named Brooks Brown in the parking lot. Brown told Harris he had missed a test in one of his classes, but, as Brown later recalled, it didn't seem to make any difference to him. Then Harris looked at Brown. "Brooks, I like you," he said. "Now get out of here. Go home."

After Brown had departed, Harris and Klebold took two large duffel bags from their cars and walked into the school cafeteria. They set the bags down beside a lunch table. No one noticed as the two friends then left the cafeteria and returned to their cars. Nor did the duffel bags themselves attract any attention. Hundreds of students crowding into the cafeteria to eat lunch left their backpacks and bags on the floor. But while the

The Columbine shooters.
This page: Eric Harris.
Facing page: Dylan Klebold.

backpacks of the other kids contained notebooks and calculators and pens, Harris and Klebold had loaded their duffel bags with 20-pound propane tanks, which they had fashioned into homemade bombs. They had set the bombs to explode at 11:17.

The time wasn't random. With the detachment and attention to detail of a scientist, Harris had earlier observed the "A" lunch period at Columbine. In a notebook, along with a diagram of the room, he had recorded an almost minute-by-minute count of the number of students in the cafeteria. At 11:17 the cafeteria was fullest, with more than 500 people sitting at

tables and standing in lines. Bombs that exploded then would kill the most students.

An idea like slaughtering one's classmates doesn't simply occur overnight, and Eric Harris may have started the long journey that led to April 20, 1999, many years earlier. As an elementary school student, he seemed to have trouble fitting in and finding a comfortable place for himself among his peers. His father, Wayne, was a highly successful U.S. Air Force pilot, and the Harris family moved frequently from one base to another. Eric Harris later recalled how hard it had been to continually begin again "at the bottom of the ladder."

In 1993, Wayne Harris retired from the military after 20 years of service, moved his family to Littleton, and took a civilian job training pilots. But this additional element of stability didn't appear to make life any easier for Eric Harris. He never seemed capable of measuring up to his father or his older brother, who had been a football star at Columbine before going on to college. Ironically, Eric Harris often found himself being picked on by the jocks at Columbine, who formed the most prestigious clique in the school. The taunts became even worse in Eric's junior year, when he joined a small group of students who dressed in long, dark coats and called themselves the Trench Coat Mafia.

Despite early news reports to the contrary, the Trench Coat Mafia wasn't a gang. Rather, it was, according to a report by the Jefferson County, Colorado, sheriff's department, "a loose, social affiliation of former and current Columbine High School students with no formal organizational structure, leadership or purpose." The several dozen members spent time doing things that are fairly typical of high schoolers, such as playing video games and listening to music together, but at Columbine they were considered outcasts.

Dylan Klebold was another member of the Trench Coat Mafia. The blond, lanky Klebold seemed even shier than his friend Harris. Several years earlier, Klebold's family had moved to Littleton from Plattsburgh, New York. Thomas Klebold, Dylan's father, had decided to leave his job as a geophysicist and open a small financial-services business. Dylan's mother, Susan Klebold, worked with disabled students at a local community college. The Klebolds lived in a large, expensive house, and people who knew them said that they provided a stable home life for Dylan. But another student who knew Klebold said that "he really felt unloved." Apparently his close friendship with Harris made up for some of these negative feelings.

Soon after joining the Trench Coat Mafia, however, Harris and Klebold were arrested for breaking into a van and stealing about $400 worth of electronic equipment. Harris and Klebold were required to do community service and receive treatment in an anger management program. In February 1999, after they had completed the program, Harris was praised as a "very bright young man who is likely to succeed in life," and Klebold was characterized as "intelligent enough to make any dream a reality."

It wasn't a dream both boys were creating, however, but a nightmare. Harris had already begun to describe his dark vision on the Web page he had posted. He talked about killing the many people he resented. "God, I can't wait til I can kill you people," he wrote. "Feel no remorse, no sense of shame. I don't care if I live or die in the shoot-out. All I want to do is kill and injure as many of you as I can. . . ."

For his part, Klebold also felt a great deal of rage toward the many people he believed had taunted or slighted him, including his brother Byron and Byron's friends. "If you could see all the anger I've stored over the past four . . . years," Klebold said on a videotape he and Harris made before their attack on Columbine.

Both boys were apparently obsessed with violence and retribution. Both spent many hours playing violent video games, such as Doom and Quake. Harris even designed his own video game, which he posted on his website. It showed two people shooting their enemies. In English class, where the boys sat side by side, they regularly wrote poetry that seemed to reflect a morbid fascination with death. Klebold and Harris also took a video class together. For an assignment in that class they created a violent production in which they pretended to kill other people in a hail of gunfire.

Friends described both boys as obsessed with the German dictator Adolf Hitler and Nazism. When they went bowling, they would greet each other with the Nazi salute "Sieg Heil!"

At least a year before the massacre at Columbine, the boys had begun planning their act of revenge against the jocks and other students who had picked on them at school. For the massive assault they had in mind they would need firepower. They made the two large propane bombs and dozens of smaller pipe bombs and Molotov cocktails. On the weekend before the attack took place, both boys were in the garage at Eric Harris's home smashing bottles. The shards of glass were probably used as shrapnel for some of the bombs. Although they were making enough noise to be heard by neighbors, Harris's parents never seemed to have realized what was going on in their own garage. Nor did they see the gun that their son had hidden under his bed.

Neither Eric Harris nor Dylan Klebold was old enough to possess a handgun or to buy, from a licensed dealer, a rifle or shotgun. Yet the two still managed to amass a deadly arsenal. An 18-year-old friend, Robyn Anderson, bought two shotguns and a carbine at a gun show, then resold them to Harris and Klebold. Gun shows, which are attended by as many as five million people each year, are largely unregulated. Dealers can sell to anyone who is old enough, and because gun show dealers aren't federally licensed, purchasers can legally resell the weapons to minors. Klebold also bought a semiautomatic 9-mm handgun from an acquaintance, Mark Manes. This sale was illegal, and Manes received a prison sentence after pleading guilty to weapons charges. Harris and Klebold may have saved money to pay for the weapons from the part-time jobs both boys held at a local pizza parlor.

On April 20, 1999, the boys' preparations finally culminated in what they called Judgment Day. After planting the propane bombs in the cafeteria, they went to their cars, collected their guns and pipe bombs, and waited for the explosion. Their plan, apparently, was to gun down survivors fleeing the blast in the cafeteria.

However, things didn't go as the killers had planned.

Faulty wiring prevented the propane bombs from exploding. Around 11:20 the boys decided to launch their assault anyway. Descending a hill from the parking lot toward the school building, Harris and Klebold opened fire. Two students eating lunch on the grass outside the school library were the first casualties. Rachel Scott was killed and Richard Castaldo seriously injured.

Next, three students who had just exited the cafeteria by a side door were hit. Klebold walked down a flight of outside stairs to the area where they lay. At close range he shot and killed Daniel Rohrbaugh. He also shot Lance Kirklin again, but Kirklin survived. As a group of students sitting on the grass nearby ran for cover, the gunman fired after them, seriously wounding one boy.

Elsewhere outside the school building and in the cafeteria, students and teachers initially didn't know what was going on. Some thought that the commotion was a senior prank or part of a student video production.

"I looked up and saw the backs of two guys in black trench coats," student Melissa Miller said later. Bullets hit her friend, Anne Marie Hochhalter. "She didn't get up," Miller recalled. "She just stayed crumpled on the ground."

"This is what we always wanted to do," one of the killers was heard to say. "This is awesome!" In addition to firing their guns, Harris and Klebold also lit some of their homemade bombs, tossing them onto the school roof and into the parking lot.

When Neil Gardner, a sheriff's deputy and community resource officer at Columbine High School, arrived on the scene, Harris fired about 10 shots at him. Gardner returned fire but didn't hit Harris and didn't pursue him when the young gunman entered the school building, joining Klebold. The officer's training told him that in a crowded area like the school, a gun battle could injure or kill many innocent bystanders. Plus, Gardner needed to establish a perimeter around the building—both to help wounded and trapped students get to safety and to prevent the gunman from escaping.

Meanwhile, calls had gone out to the local police, who began arriving outside the building. But the police hesitated to enter Columbine because they didn't know how many shooters were in the building or where they were located. One wrong move by a police SWAT team might jeopardize the lives of hundreds of students.

Inside the building, Harris and Klebold were firing their weapons down the hallway as students ran into bathrooms, labs, and classrooms and locked the doors. One of the gunmen shot Dave Sanders, a business teacher who was helping students to safety, just as Sanders was about to round a corner. Another teacher helped Sanders into a classroom where a group of students was hiding. Unfortunately, he would later die from his wounds—the only teacher to be killed in the massacre.

Inside Columbine's library, teacher Patti Nielson had made a 911 call and left the phone off the hook when she hid under the front counter. Thus, investigators have an audiotape of what happened in the library. Nielson had been a hall monitor when Harris and Klebold entered the school with their guns firing. She raced to the library to warn students there: "There's a guy with a gun! Kids, under the table! Kids, stay on the floor. Oh, God. Oh, God—kids, just stay down," Nielson pleaded.

The 911 tape shows that the gunmen walked up and down the hallway outside the library, firing their guns and lighting bombs, for about two minutes. At 11:29, they entered the library, where 56 people were trying to hide. Over the next seven minutes, Klebold and Harris murdered 10 students and wounded 12 more. They fired out the library windows at law enforcement agents who had arrived and at students who had fled the building.

Then they left the library and wandered down the

I. 11:57:20-63 AM   04/20/99

Videotape from the cafeteria's surveillance camera shows Harris (left) and Klebold near the end of their deadly rampage at Columbine.

hallway toward the science area. Witnesses reported that Harris and Klebold looked through windows into locked classrooms, sometimes even making eye contact with the students taking refuge inside. But they made no attempt to get into the classrooms to murder any more people. The official report on the Columbine massacre characterized the two killers' behavior at this point as "directionless."

Outside, ambulances had begun arriving to treat wounded students. Worried parents had also rushed to the school as they received word of what was

A student signs one of the memorial crosses erected for the Columbine victims.

happening. Soon local TV stations would begin hours of uninterrupted coverage from Columbine.

For the police, however, the situation remained unclear: 911 calls from inside the building placed gun-men in different locations, and no one knew how many shooters were involved. At one point it was believed that one shooter had left the building, a development that would have created danger for the many people on the school grounds. Plus, smoke had set off sprinklers and fire alarms inside the building, making it difficult to hear where shots were coming from.

Ultimately SWAT teams entered the high school and painstakingly cleared hallways to allow students safe avenues of escape. By 3:30 P.M., when officers reached the library, Klebold and Harris had been dead for more than three hours. After moving from the science area, they had gone to the cafeteria—now empty except for a handful of students hiding in the food-preparation area—where they had stopped to drink some water and attempted to detonate the unexploded propane bombs by shooting at them. "Today the world's coming to an end," a witness heard one of the boys say. "Today's the day we die." After exploding a bomb and causing a fire in the cafeteria, Klebold and Harris had returned to the library. There, in the midst of most of the bloodshed, they had committed suicide around 12:08.

The nightmarish violence unleashed by the two boys had left 13 innocent victims dead and another 23 wounded. It had also left the community of Littleton in mourning—and the entire nation in stunned disbelief. Those who knew the boys personally and those who merely read or heard news reports about the Columbine massacre struggled to understand why it had happened. What depths of rage could have motivated the killers to behave as they did? Had the boys really been picked on mercilessly, or were there other factors that might help explain their murder spree? What sort of culture could produce these kinds of kids? More generally, what causes young people to commit violent crimes, and is the incidence of violence in schools, families, and communities increasing? What role can parents and society play in preventing children from committing acts of violence? Chapters two through seven will address these questions.

THE DARK
SIDE OF YOUTH

est friends Nathan Leopold and Richard Loeb seemed to have everything, including bright futures. The sons of millionaire businessmen, both youths led lives of wealth and privilege. Both were also highly intelligent. Leopold, who spoke nine languages, had graduated from the University of Chicago at age 18; Loeb had graduated from the University of Michigan at 17. Both contemplated a career in the law.

On a bright day in May—when the two friends were about the same age Eric Harris and Dylan Klebold would be when they went on their shooting rampage at Columbine High—Leopold and Loeb drove a rented car to the Harvard Preparatory School. Located in the same fashionable Chicago neighborhood as the boys' homes, Harvard Prep was an exclusive school where many of the city's wealthy elite sent their children.

Leopold and Loeb tried to follow a student named John Levinson, but the young boy walked up an alley

As a child Richard Loeb (shown here) is said to have fancied himself a master outlaw. Years later, Loeb would join his friend Nathan Leopold in one of the most shocking crimes of the 20th century.

and disappeared. Driving along a nearby street, they spotted 14-year-old Bobby Franks, a distant relative of Loeb's. Bobby accepted their offer of a ride home. One of the youths—authorities would come to believe it was Loeb—rode in the backseat with Bobby while his partner drove the car through the streets of Chicago. Suddenly the youth in the backseat stabbed Bobby several times in the head with a chisel, bound the dying boy with ropes, stuffed cloth into his mouth to prevent him from crying out, and covered his body with a robe.

While the body lay in the backseat of the unlocked car, Leopold and Loeb stopped at a restaurant for sandwiches. A short time later, still hungry, they stopped at another restaurant and ate a full meal.

When nightfall arrived, they drove to a swampy area near some train tracks. There the murderers poured acid on their victim's face to make identification more difficult and stuffed the body into a culvert (a large drainage pipe). Although Bobby Franks was already dead, Leopold and Loeb sent a ransom note to his father demanding $10,000 for the safe return of the boy.

By the time that note arrived, however, Mr. Franks and the police knew that Bobby wasn't going to be returned safely. A worker had spotted a foot sticking out of the culvert, and after the body was uncovered, members of the Franks family identified it as Bobby's.

Near the culvert, police also found a clue that would help them break the case: a pair of unusual eyeglasses. Contacting the manufacturer, detectives discovered that the horn-rimmed frames had been specially made for only three customers, one of whom was a certain Nathan Leopold. Soon a trail of clues pointed to Leopold and his friend Richard Loeb, and under intense questioning the youths finally confessed.

The sensational case made national headlines. Brutal as the crime was, what shocked people most was its senselessness. The murderers didn't need the money; the ransom note was simply to throw the police off their trail. Nor did Leopold and Loeb care about the identity of the boy they killed; they had discussed several possible victims and would have murdered John Levinson had they been able to get him into their car. Leopold and Loeb's only motive was that they wanted to commit the perfect crime—just for the thrill of it.

The story of the "thrill killers" Nathan Leopold and Richard Loeb has an all-too-familiar ring, as though it could have been snatched from today's headlines. The existence of wantonly murderous, apparently conscienceless youths seems an ill unique to contemporary society. In fact, Leopold and Loeb committed their crime more than 75 years ago, on May 21, 1924. Society may have undergone profound changes since that day, but then, as now, some youths—and even some young children—have shown themselves capable of the most horrific acts of violence.

Indeed, it seems that even the earliest human societies acknowledged the problem of violent children. More than 3,700 years ago, when the Babylonian king Hammurabi set down one of the first-known codes of laws, the code contained a reference to children who violently rebelled against the social order, which dictated that a father was the undisputed head of the family. The Code of Hammurabi prescribed harsh punishment for these acts. "If a son strike his father," it stated, "one shall cut off his hands."

Much later, during the Middle Ages, children who committed crimes were generally treated like adults. A child found guilty of theft or murder could be hanged. Indeed, one English law stated: "An infant of eight yeares of age, or above, may commit Homicide, and shall be hanged for it. . . ." In practice, however, many officials believed that children under 14 years old were generally too young to be responsible for their behavior. There are no statistics about the number of violent crimes actually committed by children during the Middle Ages. But the fact that governments had laws to

Engraving based on a painting by the Italian artist Raphael (1483–1520). Note the angels' baby faces, reflecting the view of children as innocent and pure.

deal with this type of crime indicates that the problem must have existed.

For a long time, European society seemed to hold conflicting images of childhood. During the 17th century, for example, some religious leaders believed that a child was born in a state of sin, which explained why certain children exhibited antisocial behavior. Parents were told that they had a duty to remove the sinfulness from their children—or the children might grow up to become criminals. By contrast, other thinkers were convinced that a baby was pure and innocent. Reflecting this notion, artists often portrayed angels as round, beautiful babies with sweet, smiling faces. A third view of childhood was expressed by the English philosopher John Locke (1632–1704). Locke believed that a baby was neither innately sinful nor innately good, but rather was born unformed, like a lump of clay. Parents could shape and mold their children to do good or evil.

No matter which view they believed, most parents recognized that children needed discipline to grow up properly. Discipline would be necessary to remove sinfulness, prevent an innocent baby from falling into evil ways, or shape an unformed child into a law-abiding adult. Often this discipline was applied harshly. Whether children were born to noble parents or peasants, they were whipped to keep them on the straight and narrow path. King Henry IV of France, for example, believed that his son—the future Louis XIII—should receive regular beatings to instill a sense of discipline and respect for his father. One mother explained that when her four-month-old child misbehaved, "I whipped him til he was actually black and blue, and until I *could not* whip him any more. . . ."

Today hardly anyone would claim that a four-month-old is capable of intentionally misbehaving. And in most quarters delivering regular beatings to a child of any age is now classified as child abuse. Of course, parents from previous eras didn't beat their children simply out of cruelty. Lacking our knowledge of psychology and child development, they believed that in the long run it would benefit the child.

During the 17th century, parents also began to see the benefit of education, and those who could afford it tried to provide more years of schooling for their children. Until this time, children had started to work on farms or as apprentices in shops by the age of seven. Gradually, the years of schooling began to increase because parents believed that education might enable their children to become more successful.

However, school could be a harsh place, especially if a child misbehaved. Many teachers seemed to believe that misbehavior was a sign of the evil that lurked inside every child. As one schoolmaster put it: "Because of the need to hold in check this age inclined to evil and not to good, often take occasion to discipline the little children, but not severely. Frequent yet not severe whippings do them good. . . ."

When English colonists came to North America,

they naturally brought with them Old World attitudes about children. Like many people in Europe, the Puritans who settled in New England, for example, seemed to hold conflicting views about the nature of childhood. Some thought that a child's heart was naturally evil, while others probably agreed with the British writer John Earle, who believed that a child's "soul is yet a white paper unscribbled with observations of the world . . . he knows no evil." No matter what parents believed, they were strongly advised to discipline their children, both to eliminate willfulness and to instill the value of self-control. The Puritans were establishing a new community in the harsh American wilderness. Their very survival depended on everyone working together and acting responsibly. As in European society, children were expected to respect their parents. Puritan law called for any child over 16 to be executed if he hit his parents, unless they had treated him cruelly or neglected his education.

New England parents strongly believed that education would instill a sense of self-discipline in children and eliminate any irresponsible behavior. Schoolteachers were encouraged to use a ruler or whip if a child misbehaved. The following lines could be found in a primer that was used to teach the ABCs:

F   The Idle *Fool*
    Is Whipt at school.
J   *Job* feels the Rod
    Yet blesses GOD.

The view that children were naturally evil and needed harsh discipline to keep them on the right path continued to be popular throughout the 18th and 19th centuries. Instead of whippings, however, more and more parents used other forms of punishment. If children misbehaved, parents might try to make them feel guilty with harsh words, send them to their rooms,

In earlier times, frequent beatings were thought to be good for children.

or even lock them in a dark closet. Parents often frightened their children with images of vicious criminals or bloodthirsty pirates, like the pirate captain Blackbeard. Parents would tell their children that these terrible men would come and take them away if they misbehaved. Many parents seemed to agree with child-rearing expert Hannah Moore, who wrote: "Is it not a fundamental error to consider children as innocent beings, whose little weaknesses may, perhaps, want some correction, rather than as beings who bring into

For generations boys have played with toy guns, seemingly without increasing their propensity for later violence.

the world a corrupt nature and evil dispositions. . . ?"

If they needed any proof of this statement, adults had only to read about conditions in London, where a survey in 1815 showed that the city was being overrun by juvenile criminals who were robbing citizens. In 1828, New York set up the first home for juvenile delinquents, who were locked away with a ball and chain around their legs to keep them off the streets. Many parents feared that their own children might fall into a life of crime unless they received proper discipline at home and in school.

Running side by side with this view, however, was a different approach to childhood made popular by the French philosopher Jean-Jacques Rousseau (1712–1778). In his novel *Émile*, Rousseau portrayed children as naturally good. He also told parents that a gentle hand could enable a child to develop this goodness. In the last half of the 19th century, many parents seemed to agree with Rousseau. Children became the center of the family. Parents began keeping baby books, where they recorded a child's growth and development. Toys—like dolls, miniature soldiers, and building blocks—were being produced by the thousands so children could play with them. And children were featured in paintings of the period dressed in white clothing, which symbolized innocence and purity.

However, parents did not lose sight of the importance of discipline. They believed that society could easily fall apart unless everyone obeyed the rules. The Reverend Horace Bushnell urged parents to instill proper values in their children by serving as positive role models. Families were also encouraged to pray with their children daily and attend church each Sunday. And as a last resort, parents were urged to instill proper values by force. One woman recalled that the best way to deal with her children was to "whip and pray and pray and whip." Gone, for the most part, was the view of children as intrinsically evil, but parents still believed that kids were capable of doing evil. And their beliefs were periodically confirmed.

During the early 1870s, for example, the city of Boston found itself gripped by a rash of horrifying crimes. Someone was enticing boys to out-of-the-way locations, then tying them up, beating them senseless, and stabbing them with a knife. The trail of evidence finally led police to a 12-year-old, Jesse Pomeroy. He was eventually convicted on the testimony of frightened victims and sentenced to prison. Less than two years later, however, Pomeroy was released on parole. Shortly afterward, two children—a boy and a girl—were brutally murdered. Police found the murder weapon at Pomeroy's house, and the young man confessed that he had committed the crimes. This time, authorities took no chances, and Pomeroy was sent to prison for the rest of his life.

Sigmund Freud, considered the founder of modern psychoanalysis, believed that parents must help develop their children's superego, or conscience.

In 1886, newspapers told the story of another 12-year-old murderer. In this case, the killer was a girl, Marie Schneider, who lived in Berlin, Germany. Schneider had pushed a little child to her death out a window. Finally brought to trial, she was convicted and sent to prison for eight years.

Ordinary people struggled to make sense of how children like Jesse Pomeroy and Marie Schneider ended up committing evil acts. Near the beginning of the 20th century, a developing science, psychology, sought to provide some answers. In some cases these answers sounded quite familiar. Granville Stanley Hall (1844–1924), considered the founder of child psychology, wrote that childhood was a period when the good inside a child battled with the evil. Most parents believed that the good would win out, if they provided their children with proper guidance and support.

Historians have called the 20th century the "century of the child"—the fulfillment of whose every need was the supposed focus of the family. As one textbook on family living pronounced: "Parents are completely responsible for their children's health, both mental and physical." Although this was probably a bit of an oversimplification, parents were expected to provide their children with the best of everything—from food and clothing to playthings and educational opportunities.

Childhood seemed to be a period of infinite possibilities, but only if parents did their part to help a child grow and develop successfully. Adults were advised that their love was necessary to help a child build a positive self-image, and that their guidance was essential to instill a proper direction for a child's future.

The Austrian psychiatrist Sigmund Freud (1856–1939) emphasized the importance of nurturing children. However, Freud also cautioned that children were multifaceted personalities, and parents must keep this fact in mind as they tried to raise them. According to Freud, the human personality includes an *id, ego,* and *superego.* A child's id includes unconscious, selfish desires for pleasure—to get what the child wants, when he or she wants it, and often at the expense of everyone else. The ego is the child's rational self, which helps determine an acceptable way to achieve desires. For example, the ego controls an individual's aggressiveness in trying to achieve his or her goals. Finally, the superego is an individual's conscience, which also keeps the id under control. Part of the responsibility of every parent, Freud believed, was to develop the child's conscience and instill a set of positive values so the child could become a productive member of society. These values were clearly absent in children who committed violent crimes—children like Jesse Pomeroy and Marie Schneider, or, more recently, Eric Harris and Dylan Klebold.

But that rather self-evident statement leads to more difficult questions: Did the families of these youths fail them? Was society to blame for their violence? Or did these youths have some unique personality characteristics that caused their violent crimes? Are murderous kids born or made—or does their behavior stem from a combination of genetic and environmental factors? If violent children have always been around, are their numbers greater in modern society? What factors might account for differences across time and culture? Social scientists continue to grapple with these questions.

Juvenile Violence: Individual, Community, and Cultural Factors

3.

In 1996, officials in Contra Costa County, across the San Francisco Bay east of the city of Oakland, investigated a stomach-turning crime. A month-old infant had been found with its head nearly smashed in by a blunt object. Fortunately, the infant survived the assault.

Such crimes often turn out to be cases of child abuse committed by a parent, another relative, or a caregiver. In this instance, however, investigators were astonished when they discovered that the attacker was a six-year-old boy. He and two eight-year-old twins had sneaked into the infant's home with the intention of stealing a bike. Then, for no apparent reason, the six-year-old viciously struck the infant in the head with a hard object.

What could cause a child so young to commit such a horrible act? One popular image of the violent juvenile is of a deranged killer who seems to murder because of mental illness. It's true that some violent

A police officer patrols the crime- and drug-ridden section of North Philadelphia known as "the Badlands." The chances that a child will commit acts of criminal violence increase if the community in which he or she lives is plagued by social disorder and crime.

juveniles (like some violent adults) do suffer from mental illness, which may be linked to brain damage or to a chemical imbalance. But most do not. (And most people with mental disorders aren't violent.) According to Dr. Martin Blinder, a psychiatrist appointed by the juvenile court to examine the six-year-old in Contra Costa County, the boy "certainly didn't exhibit any obvious evidence of a mental disability. He seemed . . . charming—a reasonably bright young man, who did a terrible thing, that didn't seem to bother him that awfully much."

Dr. Blinder believed that heredity largely explained the boy's propensity for violence. "There is something to be said for the phrase 'natural born killer,'" he remarked. "It's my view that most of what I found was predestined by his genetic endowment."

If Dr. Blinder's assessment is indeed correct, most social scientists would consider this case very much the exception. Heredity may make certain children more likely to become violent. For example, differences in brain functioning that could predispose an individual to aggressiveness and impulsiveness—contributors to much violent behavior—may be genetically linked. But environmental factors—for example, the child's family circumstances and the community in which he or she lives—seem to play an essential role also. "There is a growing consensus," asserts Patrick Tolan, an assistant professor of psychology and director of research at the Institute of Juvenile Research, "that it is a mix of inherited and other biological factors with environmental influences over time that leads to patterns of behavior that include criminal violence."

Most juvenile homicides—indeed, most acts of criminal violence by people of any age—are committed by males. This can probably be explained in part by the different ways boys and girls are socialized. Typically, girls have been taught that aggressive behavior is "unladylike" and to be avoided, and girls tend to internalize their anger. Boys, on the other hand, are often encouraged to stick up for themselves in physical confrontations; they are more likely to give vent to their anger and more likely to act impulsively. And at least one study shows that most juvenile homicides are committed on impulse.

Yet social factors probably don't tell the whole story. As Dr. Dorothy Lewis, an eminent psychiatrist and expert on violent behavior, notes, males tend to have a "diminished violence threshold, and this characteristic is true of most animals as well as man. What is it about the male constitution that creates this tendency to respond aggressively? Given the fact that this quality of temperament is not peculiar to humans, but rather is equally characteristic of animals, it makes sense to conclude that physiological rather than simply societal influences are at play." Specifically, Lewis believes, boys "are, from the outset, more susceptible than girls to . . . aggression-promoting [environmental] effects" because their bodies "secrete large amounts of androgens [male hormones] in response to particular stimuli." Androgens act on areas of the brain that control mood, and high levels of these substances may produce aggressive behavior.

Still, it's important to note that, despite recent well-publicized incidents of murderous youth, the vast majority of boys are not criminally violent. One famous study tracked all the boys born in 1945 who lived in Philadelphia between their 10th and 18th birthdays. The study revealed that just 6 percent of the boys were responsible for half of the crime and two-thirds of the violent crime committed by the entire group—a finding that has been replicated in studies of other generations of youth, and in other cities. But even among the criminally oriented 6 percent, most aren't repeat, violent offenders. Unfortunately, some criminologists believe that the level of criminality and violence has increased with each successive generation. In other words, while the proportion of criminally oriented boys has remained constant at around 6 percent since the earliest studies, the amount of serious and violent crime committed by those 6 percent has grown substantially. Princeton University political scientist John J. DiIulio, for example, cites studies indicating that each successive generation of crime-prone boys has committed three times more crime than the previous generation.

The question is, what could account for this escalating crime and violence? Many people would point the finger at deteriorating social conditions, particularly in the poorest inner-city communities. Indeed, in the past many people seemed to think that juvenile violence happened only in poor inner-city neighborhoods. Clearly this is not true, as the Columbine massacre and other recent high-profile cases demonstrate. Nevertheless, juvenile violence is at least partly an urban problem. For example, five major cities—New York, Los Angeles, Detroit, Houston, and Chicago—account for 25 percent of America's juvenile homicides.

Various factors might contribute to this phenomenon. In large cities, particularly in the poorest neighborhoods where minorities are concentrated, many children grow up surrounded by violence. Professor Arlene Stiffman of Washington University studied almost 800 teenagers in St. Louis. She reported that 50 percent had seen a killing or serious beating; and the same number said that a murder had been committed in their neighborhood. Among these same young people, 50 percent said they had been in a vicious physical fight, while one-third had used a weapon while fighting. Similar results were found in a study of youth in school in New Haven, Connecticut, during the 1990s. Almost 33 percent had seen a shooting or stabbing in their neighborhood. As a result, according to the study, these same young people experienced depression, anxiety, and a greater willingness to participate in physical fights. Surrounded by a violent atmosphere, young people

often turn to violence themselves.

In fact, University of Pennsylvania sociologist Elijah Anderson has described a "code of the streets" in which violence is the main tool for gaining respect among one's peers. This code of behavior, which prevails in the most impoverished African-American neighborhoods of the inner city, dictates that any perceived slight or act of disrespect—no matter how trivial—be met with an immediate, aggressive, and, if necessary, violent response. Thus an offense as minor as maintaining eye contact for too long becomes a reason to fight, and perhaps even to kill. On the streets,

A street fight, Harlem, New York. In some inner-city neighborhoods, violence is the main tool for gaining the respect of peers, and a boy who shows himself unwilling to fight risks continual victimization.

With more than 200 million privately owned firearms, the United States might be the most heavily armed society in history. Even high-powered, fast-firing, and military-style weapons like some of those shown here may be purchased legally.

respect is not simply a matter of status, but of survival. Those who have earned it, and who continue to deal forcefully with any new threats, have earned the right to be left alone. Those who show themselves unwilling to fight when "disrespected" are apt to be repeatedly victimized. This might partially explain the especially high murder rate among young black men. Although African-American males between the ages of 14 and 24 make up only 1 percent of the U.S. population, they commit 30 percent of all homicides. Though girls in the inner city (as elsewhere) are less violent than boys, Anderson and others have noted the emergence of a "hard-core segment" who seem to have adopted the code of their male counterparts.

Ultimately the violent code of the streets reflects a deep gulf between the urban poor and mainstream society and its values. For many inner-city youth, there seems little reason to do the things that are supposed to lead to success in America: staying in school, abiding by the law, and aspiring to find a good job. In their impoverished communities, good jobs don't exist. In short, there seems little hope for any future. Indeed, as political scientist John DiIulio has written, "[A]sk a group of today's young big-city murderers for their thoughts about 'the future,' and many of them will ask you for an explanation of the question."

Delinquency, Travis Hirschi explains in his book *The Causes of Delinquency*, occurs "when an individual's bond to society is weak and broken." Certainly the bond to society of those caught inside the impoverished inner cities is often weak. Statistics show that during the 1990s, a period of enormous economic expansion, 22 percent of America's young children still lived in poverty. Reforms forced the parents of many of these children off the welfare rolls and often into very low-paying jobs. Indeed, a study by the Center on Budget and Policy Priorities shows that while the number of poor children has declined in recent years, those left behind are poorer than ever. In a society that puts enormous value on money and what it can buy, poor children tend to suffer from low self-esteem and from a sense of hopelessness. Sociologist Robert Merton believes that, in the absence of acceptable ways to achieve the goals that Americans regard as important, youth may turn to delinquency.

Drugs are another factor that might help explain the high rates of juvenile violence—and in particular, juvenile homicide. According to one study, 20 to 25 percent of kids who kill were high on alcohol or drugs when they committed their crimes. In addition, the drug trade itself has spawned much juvenile violence. Crack cocaine, for example, was introduced into the nation's cities during the 1980s. This highly addictive, relatively inexpensive, smokable form of cocaine quickly became the drug of choice in urban areas. Where there's a large market, there's money to be made; and where there's money to be made, there's usually stiff competition. Drug gangs battled one another for a share of the lucrative crack trade, and the "soldiers" in these wars were often teenagers. Of course, they had to be well armed. As a result, America's cities witnessed a seemingly endless string of juvenile killings, often in the form of drive-by shootings. Eventually, after much bloodshed, the stronger and more ruthless gangs eliminated the weaker gangs, and the crack wars subsided. But all the firepower that had been used in those wars remained—along with a culture in which guns are readily accepted as a legitimate means to solve problems. It's no coincidence, experts believe, that between 1984 and 1994, when the number of juvenile homicides tripled, the number of juvenile homicides committed with guns also tripled.

Despite laws that prohibit minors from buying or selling them, guns are often readily available to young people, who can buy them from drug dealers or friends. A cheap handgun can be purchased for as little as $20; an automatic weapon might cost $100. Experts believe that juvenile felons in urban areas are much better armed than they were even 10 years ago, and this is a major factor in the number of juvenile killings. In one study of 750 students from 10 inner-city public schools, 45 percent said they had been threatened by someone with a gun or actually shot at as they traveled to or from school. Many of these students believed they needed guns to protect themselves.

Of course, it's not just in urban areas that guns are easily available. In fact, a survey conducted by the Centers for Disease Control and Prevention revealed

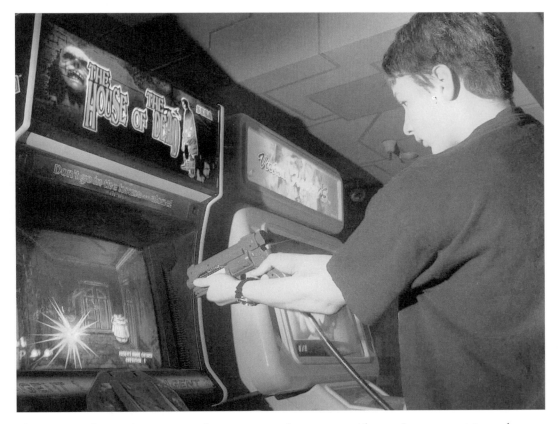

that more than 18 percent of young people nationwide carried a weapon. And Arkansas, Louisiana, Texas, and Oklahoma lead the nation in teenage homicides. In rural areas especially, many kids grow up knowing how to shoot because target shooting and hunting are popular family pastimes.

The American Institute of Justice estimates that approximately 200 million firearms are privately owned in the United States. These include rifles, handguns, and semiautomatic assault weapons, like the AK-47. The availability of guns makes it easier for teenagers to use them to commit a crime. In Littleton, Colorado, for example, Dylan Klebold and Eric Harris had no trouble getting weapons from friends who had purchased them at a gun show. Other juvenile killers simply take guns from their parents or neighbors. Studies show that more

Innocent activity or dangerous pastime? The vast majority of kids who play violent video games will never use a real gun against real people. But, some experts believe, such games may desensitize certain children to violence.

than 50 percent of guns are not locked up by the adults who own them, and approximately 16 percent are not only unlocked but loaded.

In the past, kids frequently settled disputes with harsh words or their fists. More and more, however, guns now enter the mix, with predictably tragic consequences.

Experts in juvenile justice have long wondered whether there is any connection between the actual violence committed by youth and the depictions of violent acts young people are exposed to in popular culture and the media. Increasingly, the evidence seems to point to a link—although this link falls far short of a cause-effect relationship. In rare instances juveniles have admitted reenacting a scene they witnessed in the movies or on television. For example, four teens who were involved in a violent sexual assault in San Francisco said they had seen a similar incident on a television program only three days earlier.

For the most part, however, the relationship between watching violence and committing it is not so direct. The average American child watches four hours of television daily and sees 40,000 murders in the media before turning 18. Obviously, only a very small proportion of kids become murderers themselves. But philosopher Sissela Bok and others believe that this exposure can still produce profound effects in children. First, they can become more afraid of being murdered, a fear that is out of proportion to the actual risk. Second, media depictions of violence may also desensitize kids to actual violence: because they are bombarded with violent images—in movies, on TV, in video games, and even in the lyrics of certain music—violence ceases to have any meaning. Third, constant exposure to media images may cause some children to believe that violence is the appropriate and expected way to solve interpersonal problems. A National Television Violence study revealed that most of the people who commit murder on TV are never punished for their crimes. Observes Leonard Eron, a psychologist at the University of Michigan and an expert on media, "The lesson they [children] learn is that everybody does it and this is the way to behave." Eron adds, "There can no longer be any doubt that heavy exposure to televised violence is one of the causes of aggressive behavior, crime and violence in society." Critics of the media also point to video games that involve killing, as well as rap music with violent lyrics. Eric Harris, for example, played violent video games, like Doom.

It must be emphasized that most young people who see violence in the media or play violent video games don't become violent themselves. But media violence may be one factor, taken along with others, that influences some young people to commit violence. As the American Psychological Association stated: "Depictions of violence in the mass media . . . may reinforce the tendency toward aggression in a young child who is already exhibiting aggressive behavior."

FAMILY VIOLENCE

In 1847, the British public was shocked to read about a terrible crime committed by 12-year-old William Alnutt. After a difficult childhood spent with a violent, alcoholic father, William had gone to live with his grandfather, Samuel Nelme. A disobedient boy who even stole money from his grandfather, William had to be punished regularly. One day Nelme became so enraged with his grandson that he pushed the boy to the floor, then banged his head against a wall. Perhaps it seemed like a repetition of the violence he'd experienced while living with his father. Whatever the case, William vowed to get even. He put some arsenic in the sugar that his grandfather used to sweeten his food. By the end of the week, the old man had died a horrible death. Police considered the death suspicious, and an autopsy revealed poisoning. William eventually confessed to the crime and went to prison for the rest of his life.

Some 145 years later, in 1992, another youngster

Domestic violence, even when it isn't directed at children, puts kids at risk for becoming violent themselves. This may be because the children model their parents' behavior and come to see violence as the way to solve problems.

49

who had killed a relative sat in an American courtroom facing a jury that would decide her fate. Since she'd been a toddler, Donna Marie Wisener's father had physically abused her. Like many fathers who abuse their children, he also beat his wife. As Donna Marie grew older, the beatings she suffered grew worse. One night, after Wisener had beaten his wife, he turned his fury on Donna Marie, then ordered her to leave the house. Later she returned home, took her father's gun, and shot him dead. In view of her father's history of physical abuse, the jury decided that Donna Marie had acted in self-defense and found her not guilty of the murder.

In part, the differing outcomes of the Wisener and Alnutt cases may reflect both changing attitudes toward parental authority and an increased understanding of the effects of abuse upon children. Child abuse has probably existed since the earliest civilizations. Of course, our modern views on what constitutes child abuse differ markedly from the views of our forebears. Treatment that we would today consider abusive—for example, repeated beatings of children to instill discipline—was in previous eras the norm.

Today we know that violence in the family—particularly when it occurs repeatedly and over a long period of time—can have severe consequences for a child's emotional and psychological development. Like violence in the community or media images of violence, it puts a child at greater risk for becoming violent. In fact, a history of child abuse is one of the primary risk factors for juvenile violence.

"Probably the most powerful generator of aggression in living beings," observes Dr. Dorothy Lewis, "is pain. Animals that have been tortured and children who have been severely and repeatedly abused often become extremely aggressive."

Displaced rage may partially explain why this is true. Because a young child is powerless to stop the person who causes the pain—the abusive parent—he or she enacts violence on others who are less powerful. Often this means other children.

Mary Bell's mother repeatedly abused her physically, even attempting to kill Mary on several occasions. And from an early age Mary herself displayed violent tendencies when she played with other children from her neighborhood in Newcastle-upon-Tyne, Scotland. Indeed, she had even grabbed two little girls by the throats and tried to choke them. In 1968, just after her 11th birthday, Mary was finally arrested for two murders. She had killed one child, four-year-old Martin George Brown, on May 25, 1968, in an abandoned house. However, the death looked like an accident, and the case was closed. Two months later, she strangled three-year-old Brian Howe, then scratched an M on his stomach with a pair of scissors. This time Mary's friend Norma Bell (no relation) told police that Mary had bragged about killing Brian. At Mary's trial, one expert testified that she demonstrated no feeling and no remorse for what she had done. Mary may have felt powerless to get back at her mother, so she took her anger out on the little children.

On the other hand, abuse may put a child at risk for later criminal violence because it undermines the child's capacity to empathize with other people. In coping with their own pain, some abused children lose the ability to recognize the pain of others. In addition, abuse may engender what psychologists term hypervigilance. This means that the abused person becomes

Mary Bell, who suffered physical abuse at the hands of her mother, murdered two younger children by the time she reached age 11. Victims of child abuse are more likely than other kids to commit acts of criminal violence.

Neglect, some experts believe, may contribute even more than physical abuse to juvenile violence.

overly attuned to possible threats—and responds with violence even when no threat exists.

If being a victim of abuse raises a child's risk of becoming violent, so too does the mere witnessing of violence in the household. Children may learn violence through modeling—that is, by imitating their violent parents. Studies of children who live in a violent family environment show that many of them begin to adopt an aggressive approach to dealing with other people. They get into fights with children at school. They may resort to physical force against someone who disagrees with them. Growing up in an atmosphere of violence, they may begin to see force as the only way to resolve problems with other people.

In one study, researchers talked to approximately 150 young people who lived in families where their fathers routinely beat their mothers. More than 80 percent of the boys who were dating said that they hit their girlfriends during arguments with them. Thus, these boys seemed to absorb the behavior they saw in their families and applied it in their relationships with other people.

Imitation of parents, even when they present negative rather than positive role models, may also help explain a startling statistic uncovered by Justice Department surveys. Almost half of all juvenile offenders committed to locked facilities have a parent or another close relative who previously served time in prison.

But if abusive, violent, or criminal parents increase

the chances for juvenile violence, they aren't the only significant family-based risk factor. In fact, some experts believe that severe neglect constitutes a greater risk than actual child abuse.

Neglect may be defined as a failure to provide for a child's basic needs. These include physical needs, such as adequate food, clothing, shelter, and medical care. They also include emotional and intellectual needs, such as nurturing and mental stimulation. The effects of physical neglect may be more readily apparent, but that doesn't mean the effects of emotional neglect are any less severe. A child who receives almost no stimulation during infancy will suffer extreme developmental delays, and possibly irreversible mental damage; the child may even die. Less severe emotional neglect may cause the child to have difficulties forming peer relationships and empathizing with other people, and it may lead to aggressive and violent behavior. Even parents who aren't neglectful but who nevertheless don't monitor their children's behavior closely, or parents who discipline their kids harshly and inconsistently, are more likely to produce violent children.

Not surprisingly, the combination of neglect and abuse creates a higher risk of juvenile violence than either factor alone. However, it bears reiterating that the vast majority of kids who suffer neglect and abuse don't become violent. As psychiatry professor Patrick Tolan suggests, the best predictors of youth violence "are more able to be used to predict who might be at-risk than . . . who will actually become violent."

Currently, there are approximately three million reported cases of child abuse and neglect in the United States each year. However, experts believe that the actual number may be twice as high. For a variety of reasons, many cases go unreported. Obviously an abusive parent will not want authorities to know about his or her conduct. Some children, especially young children, may not know that what is happening to them is wrong.

Some blame themselves for causing the mistreatment, while others don't know where to turn for help or are ashamed about what is going on in their family. Still others remain silent out of loyalty to their parents or fear of exposing them to criminal penalties.

Many abused and neglected children struggle with a host of emotional difficulties throughout their lives. These may include depression, difficulty in forming intimate relationships, poor self-esteem, and drug or alcohol dependency.

For a much smaller proportion, violence in the home leads to further acts of violence and even murder. Dr. Deborah Prothrow-Stith, the former Massachusetts commissioner of public health, writes: "I believe if all the children born in America learned at home how to manage anger and aggression non-violently, our homicide and assault rates would decline by 50 percent—maybe even 75 percent." Unfortunately, children who grow up in violent households are likely to have a deep well of anger, and they may see violence as the way to deal with problems. In some cases, their rage is directed at a parent, but it may just as easily be focused on someone outside the family.

For some kids, killing an abusive parent seems to be the only way out of their terrible predicament. For the most part, children who commit parricide—as the murder of a parent is called—are boys. (Girls are more likely to think about suicide as a way of escaping the violence in their homes.) Studies show that when a juvenile does kill a parent, most often some form of abuse has been occurring in the home for years: in more than 60 percent of the cases the murder takes place after years of regular spousal abuse, and 70 percent of juveniles who kill a parent have themselves been abused.

Typical is the case of Richard Jahnke, who for years regularly beat his wife and his son, Richard Jr., while sexually abusing the boy's sister, Deborah. Richard Jr. had tried to stop the violence by enlisting the help of his mother and even calling the police. But his father's violent behavior continued. Finally, the young man could take it no longer. One day in 1982, when his father was approaching the Jahnke home, Richard shot and killed him.

Interestingly, most boys who kill an abusive parent have never been guilty of another violent crime, and many have no history of criminal behavior at all. As Kathleen Heide writes in her book *Why Kids Kill Parents*, young people may strike out "in response to a perception of being trapped." The child may have tried to put up with the violence, or looked for help from friends or relatives to stop it. When these solutions prove ineffective, or perhaps lead to worsening violence, the child may fear death or serious injury and try to deal with these fears in the only way that seems effective—putting an end to the life of the person committing the abuse.

Often the youths feel isolated because they have tried to hide the family abuse, which cuts them off from friends to whom they might turn for understanding and support. In addition, many young people seem to have little time to form relationships. In a family where a parent is being abused, a young person may be forced to take over an increasing share of responsibilities—such as caring for younger siblings or doing household chores—because the abused parent may be psychologically and physically incapable of coping with the duties of parenthood.

In some cases, a juvenile may be encouraged by an abused parent to kill the other parent who is being abusive. In his book *When Children Kill*, Professor Charles Patrick Ewing explains that a child may be responding to past statements made by a woman that she wished her abusive husband was dead. Or the woman may do even more to encourage her child to kill his father. In one case, according to Ewing, a man beat his wife and then left the room. She turned to her son

NATIONAL
DOME
VIOLEN
OTLIN
800-799-SAFE (72.
e Deaf)

Kelly White, executive director of the Domestic Violence and Sexual Assault Survival Center, speaks at a news conference. Programs designed to help abused women also help their children.

and said, "I know you're big enough to protect me now." Then she brought him a pistol and he killed his father.

Ewing also describes a few cases in which juveniles have killed their mothers. Like killings of fathers, these murders generally occurred after repeated abuse.

Frequently, women and their children try to escape abuse at the hands of fathers or boyfriends by leaving their homes and seeking protection in shelters for battered women. These shelters have been established in many communities throughout America. Programs are available at some of them, as well as through social service agencies, to help children deal with the effects of abuse. These programs include group counseling designed to encourage children to talk about the violence that has occurred in their homes.

In addition, these children learn how to restore their sense of self-esteem, which has been brutally undermined by family violence. Many children are also prone to acting out their feelings and behaving aggressively toward their peers. The counseling programs are designed to help these children modify their behavior so they can learn to relate to others without using force.

A key to helping children heal is to help their mothers. Many of them, overwhelmed by years of abuse, may lack the patience and energy necessary to create a loving, nurturing environment for their children. Counseling is designed to enable them to learn the skills they need to create a supportive atmosphere that will allow children to rebuild their self-esteem. These parents also learn effective communication skills so they know how to listen to their children, give them praise, and instruct them in interpersonal relationships.

Dr. Prothrow-Stith, the former Massachusetts commissioner of health, adds that schools must also instruct students in proper parenting. Many young people learn how to parent by watching their own parents. If their family environment is marred by violence, they may simply repeat the cycle. "I believe that parent training ought to be a mandatory course in every high school in our nation," Prothrow-Stith writes. "Most of us become parents. Few of us are prepared for the job." As more and more young people are trained to become better parents, she believes, their children will be far less likely to resort to violence.

SCHOOL VIOLENCE

During the last half of the 1990s, the rate of violent crime among juveniles began to decline steadily after a decade-long rise. At the same time, however, many Americans got the sense that juvenile violence was worse than ever. Perhaps that was because of a rash of shocking, well-publicized shooting sprees at schools.

Like Leopold and Loeb many years before, the authors of these rampages didn't fit the typical image most Americans had of violent juveniles. They were from rural areas and middle-class suburbs; they were white; and some had intact, two-parent families. The school shooting spree itself seemed like an entirely new manifestation of youth violence. In reality, it wasn't.

Kipland Kinkel is led into court following his shooting spree at Thurston High School in Springfield, Oregon. Kinkel, who had murdered his parents the day before attacking students in Thurston High's cafeteria, claimed to hear voices in his head commanding him to kill.

On a Monday morning in January 1979, 16-year-old Brenda Spencer went to the window of her home, which stood just across the street from the Grover Cleveland Elementary School outside San Diego, California. Taking aim with a .22-caliber rifle, which she had received as a gift from her father, Brenda began firing at children in the school yard. Inside, the school principal, Burton Wragg, heard the sounds and ran outside, expecting to see someone shooting off fire-crackers. Instead he saw wounded children, crying with pain and fear. As he tried to help one of them, Wragg was fatally wounded by a bullet from Spencer's rifle. The school janitor, Mike Suchar, ran out to help Wragg. Before he could come to the principal's aid, however, Suchar was struck and killed by another bullet. By this time, police were arriving at the scene and surrounding the neighborhood. Eventually, they forced Brenda Spencer to put down her rifle, and they took the teenager into custody. Her shooting spree left two men dead and nine children wounded. When asked why she had committed the crime, Brenda could only answer, "I don't like Mondays. This livens up the day."

The incident at Grover Cleveland Elementary School in 1979 seems eerily similar to the school shootings that broke out during the 1990s in places such as Littleton, Colorado; Pearl, Mississippi; Paducah, Kentucky; Jonesboro, Arkansas; and Moses Lake, Washington. According to a *New York Times*/CBS News poll taken after the Columbine massacre, more than 50 percent of all adolescents are fearful that killings could break out in their schools. Yet the reality is that, while school shootings have garnered a huge amount of attention, these crimes are quite rare.

That isn't to say that other violent crimes at schools are rare. According to a survey by the National Center for Education Statistics, schools have ceased to be "safe places of learning." Indeed, over half of all elementary- and secondary-school principals report that violence occurs at their school each year. This violence includes about 4,000 rapes, 7,000 robberies, and 11,000 assaults with weapons. Despite the considerably higher incidence of these crimes, school shootings have been the focus of much of the discussion about violence in the nation's schools.

The spate of school shootings in the 1990s began on February 2, 1996. At 2 P.M. on that day, 14-year-old Barry Loukaitis entered a math class at Frontier Junior High School in Moses Lake, Washington. Loukaitis, carrying an assault rifle, began firing. As he killed one student, he was heard to say: "This sure beats algebra, doesn't it?" John Lane, a teacher who was conducting a class nearby, heard frightened screams and went down the hall to the math classroom to investigate. When Lane saw what was happening, he tried to calm Loukaitis and talk him into letting all the students leave. When this didn't work, Lane quickly charged the young gunman and succeeded in disarming him. By this time, however, two students and a math teacher were already dead.

Loukaitis had been heavily armed for his attack on Frontier Junior High. Besides the assault rifle, he also carried an automatic pistol and another handgun. He had no trouble obtaining these weapons from his family's gun cabinet. He had also received plenty of shooting practice with his father. Reports indicated that Loukaitis may have been trying to imitate the violence he saw in the media. One of his favorite movies was *Natural Born Killers*, which featured two mass murderers. He also enjoyed a video game in which the main character dreams about avenging himself on other students who make fun of him. According to reports, one of the victims was an athlete who had teased Loukaitis, so his motive may have been revenge. He also suffered from depression. He received two life sentences for the murders.

"I kill because people like me are mistreated every day," 16-year-old Luke Woodham claimed after he had murdered two classmates and wounded seven others. "I do this to show society—push us and we will push back."

In October 1997, just over a year after the incident at Moses Lake, the nation witnessed another tragic school shooting. This time the site was Pearl High School in the small city of Pearl, Mississippi, and the shooter was 16-year-old Luke Woodham.

Woodham had some history of violence. He had already killed his beloved dog, Sparkle, by beating the defenseless animal over the head, then lighting its body on fire. Experts point out that the killing of pets or other animals is a warning sign for later acts of violence and murder against people. Woodham also had a troubled relationship with his mother, who apparently blamed him for driving her husband away and constantly taunted him by calling him fat and stupid. In addition, he admitted that he felt like an outsider in school, where other students picked on him because they thought he was gay. "I hated, really hated the world," he said. But the trigger for Woodham's rampage may have been a breakup with his girlfriend, who seemed to be the only one who loved him.

On October 1, 1997, as his mother slept, Woodham murdered her with a butcher knife. Then he took his brother's hunting rifle and marched into school, where he killed two students, including his former girlfriend, and wounded seven others. Later, he seemed to cast his shooting spree as an act of revenge against a cruel society. "October 1, 1997, will go down in history as the day I fought back," Woodham claimed. "I kill because people like me are mistreated every day. I do this to show society—push us and we will push back." Woodham received three life sentences.

Exactly two months after Woodham's shooting spree in Pearl, another troubled teen struck in West Paducah, Kentucky. A group of students was just completing a prayer meeting inside the entrance of Heath High School when 14-year-old Michael Carneal appeared. He reached into his backpack, pulled out a .22-caliber semiautomatic handgun, and began firing. The prayer group's leader, a varsity football player named Ben Strong, reacted quickly. Strong charged Carneal and disarmed him. Unfortunately, three students were already dead and five others wounded, one of whom would be partially paralyzed.

Investigations into Carneal's background presented a mixed picture of the thin, curly-haired murderer. "He was a nice guy," said Strong, who was a friend of Carneal. "We talked a lot, and he just seemed like he was always a happy guy." Carneal was a good student and a member of the high school band. His minister, Frank Donner, added, "The first Sunday in May, Michael knelt at this altar and confessed his faith in Jesus Christ as his savior. I believed him then and I believe him now." It didn't sound like the typical profile of a juvenile murderer.

But other reports told a somewhat different story. His principal, Bill Bond, reported that Carneal "had been teased all his life" and "just struck out in anger at the world." He may have been bullied by other students at Heath High. He was also called gay in the school paper.

Carneal had stolen the pistol he used to kill his schoolmates, as well as several other firearms, from a neighbor's garage. Many people own guns in the Paducah area, where hunting is a popular pastime. However, Carneal's father—a successful lawyer—seemed to believe that his son had very little interest in guns. Nevertheless, the boy may have been influenced by a movie called *The Basketball Diaries* in which a student kills his classmates.

Members of the McCracken County, Kentucky, sheriff's department escort Michael Carneal to his arraignment on murder charges, January 15, 1998. The previous December, Carneal had shot to death three students at his high school. According to his principal, the 14-year-old "had been teased all his life."

Carneal may have considered himself emotionally unstable—he surfed the Internet using the name *Loco*. While psychiatrists who examined him said he suffered from depression, they did not see any signs of serious mental illness. Like other juvenile killers, however, he may have simply been unable to control his violent impulses, which erupted in a murderous rage. "He just lost it," Strong said. After pleading guilty but mentally ill, Carneal was sentenced to life in prison.

The next highly publicized school shooting incident, in Jonesboro, Arkansas, was particularly shocking for two reasons. First, unlike the previous incidents, this one seemed carefully planned; it was certainly not a spontaneous act of rage. Second, there was the matter of the perpetrators' ages: Mitchell Johnson was 13, his friend Andrew Golden just 11.

On the morning of March 24, 1998, Johnson stole his parents' van and drove to Golden's home. Golden's parents, who had already gone to work, probably assumed their son was on his way to school. But they were mistaken. The two boys tried to break into a locked safe where the Goldens kept several guns. When they were thwarted, the boys took some handguns that Golden's parents had left readily available in the house. Then they drove to a farm owned by Golden's grandfather, sneaked into the basement, and stole several rifles and handguns.

From the farm, the boys headed toward their school, Westside Middle School. Dressed like soldiers, they left the van and walked to a ridge about 100 yards from the building. One of them sneaked into the school and set off a fire alarm, which brought the students streaming out of the building. As they entered the school yard, sounds were heard a short distance away. "It sounded like firecrackers," one student recalled. But it was gunfire from Golden and Johnson.

At first the students in the yard couldn't believe what was happening. As one girl fell from a bullet, a friend said: "Don't worry. Don't worry. It's all fake." But the girl cried: "No, it's not. I just got shot!" One of the middle-school teachers, Sharon Wright, tried to prevent a student from getting shot by shoving her to the ground and lying on top of her. For her courageous act, Wright herself was shot. She later died from her wounds. Although the gunfire was over in two minutes, four girls and a teacher lay dead. As Golden and Johnson tried to escape, they were caught by nearby construction workers and handed over to the police.

After the shootings, experts tried to explain why the two young boys might have committed this horrible act of violence. The question of *how* they had done it was much easier to answer: getting their hands on a small arsenal of weapons had been no problem. Guns and hunting are an accepted part of life in rural Arkansas.

As Jonesboro mayor Hubert Brodell put it: "It's a sport, like fishing . . . done by husband and wife, by father and son and daughter. This is family." Andrew Golden had learned how to shoot from his father and grandfather.

As far as the boys' state of mind was concerned, Andrew Golden seemed to be doing well in school. Still, the 11-year-old was described as "mean-spirited," and he had recently been rejected by a girl.

Mitchell Johnson had been described by friends and relatives as a happy child, at least until the summer of 1997. Then, according to people who knew him, something happened. "Mitchell was bragging that he smoked heroin," said one neighbor, "and weed, that he'd joined a gang." He also enjoyed playing the video game Mortal Kombat, in which players try to kill their opponents, and he listened to gangsta rap music, which glorifies violence.

Commenting on the tragedy at Jonesboro, Arkansas governor Mike Huckabee said:

> It should not surprise us that these things happen in a culture that glorifies violence and devalues life. In our movies, our television, and our music, children are taught for hours each day that violence is easy, painless, and without consequence. . . . But it's not honest or fair to lay all of the blame at the feet of the mass media. The images children see on television don't have nearly the impact as the lessons they are taught at home. A child who grows up among violence is more likely to become violent.

"If I could go back and change what happened, I'd change it in a minute," Mitchell Johnson said. "I thought we were going to shoot over their heads. We didn't think anyone would get hurt." Was it possible that the boys did not understand what they were doing? Did they think the entire shooting was just a game? Did the boys believe they were part of a television program and the people who were hit would stand up, like actors in a show, and walk away? Juvenile Court judge Ralph Wilson Jr. apparently didn't think so. He imposed the

maximum sentence allowed by law in Arkansas: incarceration in an institution for juveniles until they reached the age of 21. Many people found that sentence woefully inadequate for kids who had taken five lives, even if the killers were so young.

But the national focus didn't remain on Jonesboro for very long. Less than two months after the murders at Westside Middle School, another shooting took place across the continent in Springfield, Oregon. On May 21, 1998, a high school freshman named Kipland Kinkel walked into the cafeteria at Thurston High School and opened fire on students who were having lunch. Two students were killed and 22 others wounded before Kinkel had to stop to reload his gun. At this point, a group of students charged Kinkel and forced him to the floor.

After the incident, people in Springfield asked the question that had become so familiar to shocked members of the other communities that had experienced a

Although the nation had already witnessed several school shootings, the March 1998 incident at Westside Middle School was particularly shocking because of the ages of the killers. Mitchell Johnson (left) was 13; Andrew Golden, 11.

school shooting: why had this terrible act of violence occurred? Some of Kinkel's classmates recalled that he had once praised Theodore Kaczynski, the Unabomber, who killed three people with letter bombs. A day before the shootings, Kinkel had been arrested when a pistol, which he had purchased from a friend, was found in his locker. But police permitted Kinkel to be taken home by his parents.

Kinkel's parents, both Spanish teachers, had become concerned about their son and tried to help him. He repeatedly made angry outbursts when he was upset and seemed fascinated by guns and bombs, so much so that his parents took him to see a psychologist. However, Kinkel received no further treatment except to be given the antidepressant Prozac. Meanwhile, classmates reported that he regularly talked about killing animals and exhibited a hair-trigger temper on the basketball court, especially if he lost a game. In his journal, he revealed negative feelings about himself and anger at several students. Apparently, Kip Kinkel was also extremely angry at his parents. During the afternoon of May 20, Kinkel went home and killed his father. Later in the day, after his mother came back from school, he killed her too. Police discovered the bodies when they went to the Kinkel home the next day, after the shootings at Thurston High School.

After he was brought into custody, Kinkel was examined by psychologists, who reported that he claimed to hear voices in his head that were driving him to kill. These hallucinations may have indicated that Kinkel suffered from mental illness. "I have to kill people," he wrote following the murder of his parents. "I don't know why. I am so sorry."

By April 1999, when Eric Harris and Dylan Klebold went on their deadly rampage at Columbine High School, the question as to why school shootings were occurring with such regularity took on renewed importance. Warning signs—depression, taunting by peers, obsession with death and violence—were identified. But definitive answers remained elusive.

They still are. Ironically, however, Harris and Klebold may have at least partially explained the recent spate of school shootings in videotapes they secretly made before their killing spree. "Do not think we're trying to copy anyone," Harris said, adding that he and Klebold got the idea of carrying out a school shooting "before the first one ever happened." Whether or not this was true, experts believe that some school shootings may indeed be the work of copycats. Just as a child raised by violent parents may come to see violence as the way to solve problems, a troubled or depressed kid may model the violent acts of peers—especially after seeing the immense media attention those acts generate.

But something else comes through clearly on Harris and Klebold's videotapes: the two killers' burning desire for celebrity. "Directors will be fighting over this story," Klebold predicted. With the limited perspective of young people, they believed that their act would bring them lasting fame and even respect. "Isn't it fun to get the respect that we're going to deserve?" Harris mused.

Concludes Mark Holstlaw, an FBI special agent who investigated the Columbine massacre, "You have two individuals who wanted to immortalize themselves. The wanted to be martyrs and to document everything they were doing."

Though it remains the deadliest, Harris and Klebold's massacre wasn't the last school shooting in the United States. In fact, just one month after they struck, a 15-year-old shot up his high school in Conyers, Georgia, wounding six.

Experts continue to look for patterns in the backgrounds of the juveniles who commit these crimes. "They [don't] fit the classic profile of an antisocial kid," explained Jeff Sprague of the Institute on Violence and Destructive Behavior at the University of Oregon, "a kid who comes from poor, criminal, drug-abusing

A police officer uses a hand-held metal detector to search a student before the student enters school. Many school districts have adopted drastic measures to curtail the threat of violence in their schools.

parents, with a history of abuse, whose first arrest was when he was [very young]." The juveniles involved in the school shootings have been different. "All these boys—at Jonesboro, Paducah, Pearl—they were all that much more hidden in that regard," Sprague added. "They didn't stick out as much."

Facing this type of threat, how can schools begin to protect themselves against juvenile violence? Some school districts have adopted a policy called zero tolerance. Violent misconduct, such as bringing a gun or knife to school, or engaging in a fistfight, results in automatic suspension or expulsion. In Chicago, for example, the number of expulsions increased from only a handful in the early 1990s to more than 600 annually by the end of the decade. Juveniles are also being written up and given detention for pushing each other or roughhousing.

Some critics believe that schools are being too harsh on young people. "We have confused aggression and violence," explains family therapist Michael Gurian. "There is nothing wrong with being aggressive. There is something wrong with being violent." But school officials believe their policy has achieved impressive results. In Baltimore, for example, criminal acts in the high schools declined by 31 percent following implementation of a zero-tolerance policy.

Other schools have increased surveillance activities that might spot a potential juvenile shooter. At Permian High School in Odessa, Texas, for instance, cameras have been set up to provide continuous pictures of the parking lot and the entrance to the school, where a teenager with a gun might be entering. Other schools have begun drills in case a shooting begins. At Schaumburg High School, outside Chicago, these drills began in 1998. When the principal announces, "We're in a lockdown situation," students immediately hit the floor and try to remain out of the line of fire. In addition, local SWAT teams patrol the school looking for weapons. Many schools have also installed metal detectors. In Boston, students who come to school with a weapon are sent to a special center where they undergo psychological testing. Then a program is designed for them that includes counseling and classes in how to deal with their anger constructively.

Other schools have tried to reduce violence by initiating programs like peer mediation. Students are specially trained to step in and work with classmates who may be about to begin a fight. At one high school in Michigan, the number of fights has declined from 40 to only 1 per year. Children as young as five years old are also learning in elementary school how to deal with their anger and resolve conflicts without fighting. A survey of students at 15 elementary schools in New York City who took classes in conflict resolution revealed that these students had learned to use negotiation and other peaceful means to deal with their conflicts.

Meanwhile, the latest statistics show a drop in school violence. In 1998, there were 25 violent deaths in and around schools, as compared to double that number in the early 1990s. Though the decline in school violence—which parallels a reduction in all violent crimes among juveniles—is encouraging, many Americans have a vague sense that the nation is failing its children.

JUVENILE JUSTICE

n late 1999, a jury in Pontiac, Michigan, convicted 13-year-old Nathaniel Abraham of murder for the killing of Ronnie Greene Jr. The killing had occurred two years earlier while Abraham, who was only 11 at the time, had been taking target practice with an old .22-caliber rifle. He climbed up a hillside, took aim, then shot Greene, who had just come out of a convenience store, in the head. According to prosecutors, the boy later boasted of the killing to friends in school. Abraham may be the youngest child ever charged with and convicted of murder in an American court.

Increasingly, however, the American public has become fed up with juvenile offenders, especially when they commit violent crimes. And the justice system has responded. Younger and younger defendants are now being tried in adult courts—and sentenced to harsh punishments that once were reserved for adult criminals.

Nathaniel Abraham and his defense lawyers at the start of Abraham's murder trial, 1999. Though he was just 11 when he shot to death a man for target practice, Abraham was charged as an adult and eventually convicted of first-degree murder.

According to a law passed by the Michigan legislature in 1996, *any* juvenile—defined as a youth under the age of 16 or 18—can be tried as an adult with a judge's permission. Although this is one of the harshest laws in the nation, many other states have passed similar legislation. A majority of states now allow juveniles as young as 13 to be tried in adult court if a special waiver is first obtained from a juvenile court judge. Whether the waiver is granted usually depends on the seriousness of the crime and the youth's ability to understand the nature of his or her actions.

The rationale behind trying violent juveniles in adult court is that the punishment will be greater if they are found guilty. Some politicians have characterized this "get tough" approach as "adult crime, adult time." A majority of states even allow juveniles guilty of murder to be executed (though a 1988 Supreme Court decision set 16 as the minimum age for an execution).

Between 1988 and 1992, the number of juveniles tried as adults rose by almost 70 percent. School shooters Michael Carneal and Kipland Kinkel, for example, were both tried as adults and given harsh sentences. Carneal, who committed his crime at age 14, was sentenced to life in prison; Kinkel, 15 at the time of his shooting spree, received a prison term of 112 years.

It wasn't always this way. Since the beginning of the 20th century, the cases of juvenile offenders had almost always been heard in special courts designed to accommodate the special needs of the wayward young. The underlying assumption was that children, even those who had committed violent crimes, could still be rehabilitated—provided they received the care they needed.

Before that, in the 1800s, various approaches were tried to solve the problem of juvenile crime. Some worked at the margins of the legal system. Though these approaches made certain social assumptions that today seem offensive, the goal was always to transform young offenders, and those considered at risk of becoming offenders, into law-abiding citizens.

During the first half of the 19th century, thousands of people fleeing poverty in Europe immigrated to the United States. Many settled in crowded, impoverished immigrant neighborhoods in cities such as New York, Boston, and Philadelphia. American reformers feared that the urban slums were breeding grounds for juvenile delinquency, but poverty, they believed, was only part of the reason why. The reformers, who came from the middle and upper classes, tended to view the much different families of lower-class immigrants as unhealthy, and these parents as generally unfit.

In 1825, the Society for the Prevention of Pauperism in New York opened the first House of Refuge. It was designed to take in children who had been abandoned by their parents or caught committing crimes. Reformers hoped the strict discipline of the House of Refuge would turn children from crime and enable them to become law-abiding citizens. Children followed a rigid schedule—beginning at sunrise every morning—that required them to wash and march into the parade yard. There they were carefully inspected. After breakfast, they went to work making shoes or spinning cotton. The long day also included time for prayer and classroom instruction. Reformers claimed that many children had turned their lives around while living at the House of Refuge. But there were also persistent reports of brutal treatment by guards.

Although houses of refuge were established in several cities, there seemed to be little reduction in the amount of juvenile crime. Some reformers concluded that the harsh environment of an institution was the wrong way to guide children away from a life of crime. Led by Charles Loring Brace, these "Child Savers," as they were called, decided that the best way to reform children—lower-class, immigrant children, that is— was to get them away from the corrupting influence of urban ghettoes and their unfit parents. "To create the true home, it was often necessary to break-up the unworthy families," one reformer explained in 1888.

The way to do that, some believed, was to load the children on trains and ship them to towns and farms in the Midwest, where they would live with "worthy" families in the healthy environment of the country-side. Brace and his supporters did manage to "save" many children in this manner. While their intentions may have been good, the Child Savers ended up creating a great deal of misery for the children. Often the Midwest families who took in the kids were merely looking for cheap labor.

In any event, the number of children sent away was never large enough to have a real impact on juvenile crime in the cities. Gradually, states and cities built more institutions, called reform schools, to deal with juveniles who committed crimes. As the name suggests, these facilities were designed to reform the lives of young people so they could become responsible adults. Some reform schools were large institutions. Others established what became known as the cottage system, in which small groups of juveniles lived and worked together under the direction of adults within the same facility. This approach was designed to create more of a family atmosphere.

Near the end of the 19th century, a group of reform-ers called Progressives began calling for sweeping changes in America. The Progressives wrote about unsafe working conditions in factories where women and children put in 12-hour days, as well as the dismal slums where millions of poor families lived. Progressives like Jane Addams believed that poverty was a root cause of juvenile crime. In 1889, Addams founded Hull House in Chicago—a community center that offered a variety of services, including educational and recre-ational programs for poor children.

Addams and other reformers also helped establish the first juvenile court system in Chicago in 1899.

Jane Addams, photographed here with a young girl, saw poverty as a root cause of juvenile crime and violence. Addams founded Hull House in Chicago in part to provide recreational and educational opportunities for poor children.

Traditionally, children accused of a crime had been treated like adults—arrested by the police, tried in an adult court, and, if they were found guilty, often sentenced harshly. The focus of the juvenile court would be different. Instead of branding juveniles as criminals, the court would try to determine the reasons why they had committed their crimes and help them find effective treatment. The purpose was to prevent these children from becoming adult criminals.

The juvenile justice system was based on an old English legal custom called *parens patriae*, the notion that the king was the father of his country. In the

HIGHWAYMAN AT 17

BURGLAR AT 17

MURDERER AT 19
HANGED AT THE TOMBS

PICKPOCKET AT 15

BURGLAR AT 18

HIGHWAYMAN AT 18

PICKPOCKET AT 13

HIGHWAYMAN AT 18

In earlier times, America's legal system treated juvenile offenders harshly. These adolescent criminals were all executed at the Tombs prison in New York City during the late 1800s.

United States, *parens patriae* came to refer to the doctrine of the state as parent. Traditionally, the state had acknowledged that not only did a child's father and mother have the right to treat the child as they saw fit, but also that they were best equipped to see to the child's welfare. Thus the law rarely interfered in family matters. But with the application of the *parens patriae* doctrine, the state was asserting that sometimes the parents didn't know what was best for the child, and in those instances the state could—and should—intervene. The juvenile court would function as a wise parent, helping kids who had gotten into trouble find their way back to the path of virtue. That, at least, was the theory.

From its beginning in 1899, the juvenile court system quickly took hold, eventually spreading from Illinois to every other state. Underpinning the juvenile justice system is the belief that children who break the law need to be treated differently from adult criminals. At each step along the way—from a police investigation to a court hearing to the disposition of the case—officials generally try to protect juveniles. Suppose the police have been called in to investigate a disturbance caused by teenagers in a neighborhood. The police officers may decide that nothing serious has occurred and, instead of bringing the juveniles to the police station, simply drive them home and tell their parents that the behavior should not be repeated. In other situations, a police officer may take a youth into custody. At this point the youth's case is reviewed by an intake officer at the police station. Here again, the officer may decide to release the young person to his or her parents with a warning. Or the parents may be advised to enroll the child in a counseling program where the child can get help dealing with his or her problems.

In more serious cases, the intake officer may recommend that a petition be filed with the juvenile court. This is similar to charging the individual with a crime.

But words like *charge* and *crime* are not used in the juvenile justice system, as a way of protecting the child. Before recommending that a child go to court, the intake officers examine a variety of factors. These might include the nature of the crime. Was it a violent crime? Has the youth been involved in other offenses in the past? Are community programs available that might help the youth? Is the family unstable and incapable of helping the child? After examining these factors, the intake officer may decide to recommend that the child go to court.

Instead of a trial, the juvenile is brought before a judge for what is called an adjudication hearing. Unlike adult criminal courts, juvenile courts don't use juries to decide guilt or innocence. In fact, in the juvenile justice system, a child is never found guilty; rather, the child is adjudicated delinquent—not in accord with the law. The difference may be largely semantic, but it nevertheless illustrates the assumptions of the juvenile system.

Before the adjudication hearing, a social worker generally investigates the youth's family and school situation, then writes a report. The report is intended to help the judge understand the youth's situation and, ultimately, decide on the best treatment option for the child should that become necessary. At the hearing, juveniles can be represented by lawyers, and prosecuting attorneys can present the evidence against the accused juvenile. After hearing all the arguments, the judge may decide to dismiss the charges, in which case the juvenile goes free. Or the judge may determine that the child is delinquent, which is not a criminal conviction. Under most circumstances the record of the proceedings is sealed, as a way to avoid stigmatizing the child later on.

A juvenile adjudicated delinquent may be assigned to a community program for treatment, but the most common decision made by judges is to place a juvenile

delinquent on probation. This enables the youth to remain in the community under the supervision of a probation officer. Beginning in 1899, Chicago created the position of juvenile probation officer to supervise young people who had come through the court system. By 1927, almost every state had a juvenile probation system. Probation officers are required to meet with juvenile delinquents regularly to ensure that they are abiding by the terms of their probation. These may include attending school regularly, not drinking alcohol or using drugs, staying away from other juveniles who are suspected of committing crimes, and not carrying a dangerous weapon. In addition, probation officers may be responsible for coordinating a treatment program for

Juvenile court chambers in Denver, early 1900s. The juvenile justice system, which originated in Chicago in 1899, is based on the premise that children who break the law should be treated differently from adult criminals.

the juvenile. This program may consist of psychological therapy, tutoring in academic courses, and career counseling. Even if a juvenile violates probation, he or she won't necessarily be taken out of the community. As one expert put it, "every effort is normally made to refrain from removing the child from the family and the community. It is not uncommon for a youth to be returned to probation status time and time again."

If the judge decides that probation or community-based treatment isn't sufficient given the nature of the offense or the character of the offender, the juvenile may be sent to a secure facility such as a reform school. Previously, most state laws stipulated that juvenile delinquents be released from reform school, and from the custody of the state, no later than their 18th or 21st birthday—regardless of what offenses they had committed. In recent years, however, many state laws have been changed to allow for longer periods of incarceration.

During the 1960s, juvenile justice reformers began putting more emphasis on keeping offenders in community-based programs and out of reform schools. Institutions were considered breeding grounds for crime. When an offender went behind bars, he or she might come into contact with more-hardened juvenile criminals. As a result, it was believed, the offender would be more likely to commit new and more serious crimes once released. By contrast, community programs enable an offender to remain in contact with family members and other supportive adults who can presumably serve as positive role models. In addition, these programs frequently offer far more than reform schools in terms of counseling and other services designed to help juvenile delinquents reform their lives.

Juvenile courts and probation officers have even tried to design community-based programs for violent offenders. Such programs might include intensive supervision by a probation officer. Under this arrangement, the probation officer might meet with the

offender several times each week and the offender might also be required to abide by a strict curfew, staying home at all times except when he or she is attending school or working at a part-time job. Other offenders live in halfway houses, group homes located in the community and supervised by on-site adult counselors. They provide serious offenders with group therapy, job counseling, and tutoring so they can finish school. In some cases, serious offenders enter a halfway house or intensive supervision following a period spent behind bars.

Each year, approximately 100,000 juveniles (about 10 percent of all those who come up for a hearing) are sentenced to incarceration in correctional centers. Sometimes called training schools or detention centers, these facilities are generally reserved for violent and

Outfitted for school: In a nationwide survey conducted by the Centers for Disease Control and Prevention, 18 percent of students admitted carrying a weapon. Many kids feel they need a gun for protection.

repeat juvenile offenders. While studies have revealed that only a small number of all juveniles are guilty of repeat offenses, this group commits about three-quarters of all violent juvenile crime.

Training schools have their supporters as well as their critics. Some critics believe that these institutions encourage violence as the strongest, most aggressive inmates often victimize the weakest. In addition, juvenile institutions seem to encourage crime. As one inmate put it: "Man, I didn't know anything about crime when I came here, but I do now." Supporters of training schools, however, point out that most juveniles sent to these institutions are already repeat or violent offenders. In addition, some violent offenders may need the regimen or discipline of a training-school environment to control themselves. Supporters also point out that some training facilities offer psychological treatment for inmates as well as programs to help them complete school and find jobs. These services may enable serious offenders to change their lives once they are released.

Nevertheless, the studies conducted of violent juvenile offenders paint a grim picture. Research shows that after they are released from institutions, 50 to 74 percent of inmates commit new crimes. This is called the rate of recidivism. For violent offenders placed on probation or into community corrections programs, the rate of recidivism has varied. In the 1970s, for example, Massachusetts closed its large training schools. Violent offenders were moved to small facilities consisting of about 30 offenders who were given counseling. After about 12 months the youths were moved to halfway houses. The rate of recidivism dropped by 50 percent among violent offenders, and those crimes they did commit were far less serious.

Other community corrections programs, however, were less successful. A study of one program showed that the rate of recidivism for violent offenders under intensive supervision was higher than for juveniles who had been put behind bars. And other studies revealed that incarceration and community corrections programs produced about the same results in terms of repeat violent crimes.

Meanwhile, many political leaders and ordinary citizens alike have called for tougher measures for dealing with juvenile offenders. They advocate trying more violent juvenile offenders as adults. The underlying philosophy of the juvenile justice system—that rehabilitating young offenders should be a primary focus—is increasingly being questioned.

FACING
THE FUTURE

The problem of violent children and adolescents isn't new and, history suggests, will never disappear completely. A minority of society's young people will commit crimes of violence, just as a minority of adults will do the same. This isn't to say that rates of juvenile violence, like crime rates in general, don't fluctuate. During the latter part of the 1990s, for example, violent crime rates among juveniles began to decline after a decade-long rise. Nevertheless, sensational incidents such as the shootings at Columbine High School occurred with enough regularity to cause Americans to wonder whether something was dramatically wrong with the nation's youth and to ponder what could be done about it.

President Clinton, with Attorney General Janet Reno seated at his left, speaks at a conference on youth violence, November 1999. The late 1990s saw a decline in juvenile crime rates, but horrifying incidents like the Columbine massacre sparked a national conversation on the causes and cures of youth violence.

The idea of severely punishing violent juvenile offenders—specifically, by locking them up for long periods—has wide appeal. Of course, this approach is guaranteed only to prevent repeat offenders. There is no evidence to suggest that tougher sentencing would have deterred, for example, school shooters Kip Kinkel or Michael Carneal, much less Eric Harris and Dylan Klebold. In addition, imposing a harsh prison sentence on a child is essentially an admission that the child cannot be reformed. Child psychologists, researchers, and other experts vehemently reject that assumption. Yet increasingly, policy makers are turning to incarceration as the primary option for dealing with violent children. As Fox Butterfield, author of *All God's Children: The Bosket Family and the American Tradition of Violence*, asserts: "This emerging national policy seems to fly in the face of research which shows that while some very young violent children are almost impossible to reform, a large number can be reformed. And the costs of early intervention are much lower than those of incarceration."

Early intervention, it must be emphasized, is no simple matter. It's true that social scientists and criminologists have identified some of the factors that put children at risk for violence. These include personality characteristics such as impulsiveness; violence, abuse, or neglect in the family; high levels of poverty, crime, social disorganization, and violence in the community; and, perhaps, cultural influences such as violent television shows, movies, video games, and music lyrics. In addition, experts say that the children most likely to become violent criminals will display warning signs— for example, habitual lying, petty theft, bullying, or cruelty to animals—by age six or seven.

Still, the vast majority of kids who exhibit these warning signs or have risk factors in their backgrounds don't become violent criminals. So while the actions of a violent juvenile can often be explained after the fact,

A teacher, coach, or mentor can make all the difference in the life of an at-risk kid.

no one can accurately predict which young people will commit violent crimes. As Kevin Dwyer, president of the National Association of School Psychologists, observed after the massacre at Columbine High School, "I know of no evaluation tool that will identify a . . . murderer" before he or she strikes.

In the absence of a way to identify the small group of children who would become violent criminals without intervention (and to focus scarce resources on them), attempts to reduce juvenile violence must take a much more general approach. Intervention efforts, many experts agree, should be directed at changing the conditions that contribute to higher rates of juvenile violence, particularly among those most at risk.

Of course, individuals such as mentors, coaches, teachers, and ministers can make a difference in the lives of individual at-risk children. "The evidence is compelling that the difference between at-risk youth who make it and those who don't is often but a single nurturing, capable adult who is there for the child on at least a predictable part-time basis," claims political scientist John DiIulio.

However, such adults aren't there for many at-risk kids, and risk factors for youth violence include notoriously intractable social problems like poverty and child abuse. Nevertheless, some experts believe that practical steps can be taken to reduce the number of violent children. Fox Butterfield cites studies indicating that "several early intervention programs, like Head Start or infant home visitation programs with trained nurses or social workers, reduce later delinquency." John D. Coie, a professor of psychology at Duke University, advocates identification of high-risk children during their preschool years and intervention through community-based programs. Any program that provides training to low-skill parents or extra nutrition or educational opportunities to their children may potentially have an impact on juvenile violence.

Others suggest that working to change attitudes toward violence may pay dividends as well. "Our research and [that of] others," notes psychiatrist Patrick Tolan, "suggests that the norms of the classroom, neighborhood, and society can promote or suppress violence among high risk children." In other words, if children receive a consistent message that violence is not an acceptable solution to their problems, they will be less inclined to commit violent acts.

Needless to say, there are no easy or total solutions to the complex and persistent problem of youth violence. But recent tragedies such as the massacre at Columbine High have raised awareness of the importance of even incremental progress toward reducing the problem.

Further Reading

Aries, Phillipe. *Centuries of Childhood*. New York: Knopf, 1962.

Barnard, Jeff. "School Killer Kept Hurt Hidden." *Los Angeles Times*, November 14, 1999.

Bartollas, Clemens, and Stuart Miller. *Juvenile Justice in America*. Englewood Cliffs, N.J.: Prentice-Hall, 1994.

Begley, Sharon. "Why the Young Kill." *Newsweek*, May 3, 1999.

Briggs, Bill, and Jason Blevins. "A Boy with Many Sides." *The Denver Post Online*, May 2, 1999.

Clement, Priscilla Ferguson. *Growing Pains: Children in the Industrial Age, 1850–1890*. New York: Twayne Publishers, 1997.

Cowley, Geoffrey. "Why Children Turn Violent." *Newsweek*, April 6, 1998.

Crime and Criminals: Opposing Viewpoints. San Diego: Greenhaven Press, 1995.

Crimes and Punishment. Westport, Conn.: H. S. Stuttman, Inc., 1994.

Davenport, John, et al. "Schools on the Alert." *Newsweek*, August 23, 1999.

deMause, Lloyd, ed. *The History of Childhood*. New York: Harper and Row, 1984.

Ewing, Charles Patrick. *When Children Kill: The Dynamics of Juvenile Homicide*. Lexington, Mass.: D. C. Heath, 1990.

Fortgang, Erika. "How They Got the Guns." *Rolling Stone*, June 10, 1999.

Gibbs, Nancy, and Julie Grace. "On March 4, Eric Harris and Dylan Klebold Sat for This Class Picture. On April 17, They Both Went to the Prom. What They Did Next Left Their School . . . in Sorrow and Disbelief." *Time*, May 3, 1999.

Goldberg, Carey, and Marjorie Connelly. "Fear and Violence Have Declined Among Teen-Agers, Poll Shows." *The New York Times*, October 20, 1999.

Further Reading

Hide, Kathleen. *Why Kids Kill Parents: Child Abuse and Adolescent Homicide*. Columbus: Ohio State University Press, 1992.

Huckabee, Mike, with Dr. George Grant. *Kids Who Kill: Confronting Our Culture of Violence*. Nashville, Tenn.: Broadman and Holman, 1998.

Johnson, Dirk. "Schools' New Watchword: Zero Tolerance." *The New York Times*, December 1, 1999.

Krisberg, Barry, and James Austin. *Reinventing Juvenile Justice*. Newbury Park, Calif.: Sage, 1993.

Kuntz, Tom. "How Carnage in Our Hallways Scarred Us, and Made Us Better People." *The New York Times*, May 23, 1999.

"Look Back in Sorrow." *Good Housekeeping,* November 1998.

Lord, Mary. "The Violent-Kid Profile." *U.S. News & World Report*, October 11, 1999.

Lurie, Stephen. "Child Psychiatrists Address Problem of Youth Violence." *The Journal of the American Medical Association*, November 24, 1999.

Media Violence: Opposing Viewpoints. San Diego: Greenhaven Press, 1999.

Pooley, Eric, and John Cloud. "Portrait of a Deadly Bond." *Time*, May 10, 1999.

Prothrow-Stith, Deborah, and Michaele Weissman. *Deadly Consequences*. New York: HarperCollins, 1991.

Roy, Maria. *Children in the Crossfire*. Deerfield Beach, Fla.: Health Communications, 1988.

Schorsch, Anita. *Images of Childhood: An Illustrated Social History*. New York: Mayflower Books, 1979.

Vaughan, Susan. "What Makes Children Kill?" *Harper's Bazaar,* September 1998.

Vito, Gennaro, et al. *The Juvenile Justice System: Concepts and Issues*. Prospect Heights, Ill.: Waveland Press, 1998.

Worth, Richard. *The American Family*. New York: Franklin Watts, 1984.

Websites

American Psychological Association
  "Warning Signs"
  http://www.helping.apa.org/warningsigns/

Centers for Disease Control and Prevention
  "Facts About Violence Among Youth and Violence in Schools"
  http://www.cdc.gov/od/oc/media/fact/violence.htm

Office of Juvenile Justice and Delinquency Prevention
  http://www.ojjdp.ncjrs.org/

"Trends in Juvenile Violence," by Dr. James A. Fox
  http://www.ojp.usdoj.gov/bjs/abstract/tjvfox.htm

Index

Abraham, Nathaniel, 73
Addams, Jane, 76
Adjudication hearings, 80
Alcohol, 43, 49, 54
All God's Children: The Bosket Family and the American Tradition of Violence (Butterfield), 88
Alnutt, William, 49, 50
American Institute of Justice, 45
American Psychological Association, 47
Anderson, Elijah, 41, 42
Anderson, Robyn, 18
Androgens, 39
Anger management programs, 17, 71
Anxiety, 40
Arkansas, 45, 65, 67
Automatic weapons, 44, 61

Baltimore, Maryland, 70
Basketball Diaries, The (film), 63
Bell, Mary, 51
Bell, Norma, 51
Berlin, Germany, 34
Blackbeard, 31
Blinder, Martin, 38
Bok, Sissela, 46
Bond, Bill, 63
Boston, Massachusetts, 33, 71, 75
Brace, Charles Loring, 75-76
Brodell, Hubert, 66

Brown, Brooks, 13
Brown, Martin George, 51
Bushnell, Horace, 33
Butterfield, Fox, 88, 90

Career counseling, 82
Carneal, Michael, 63-64, 74, 88
Castaldo, Richard, 19
Causes of Delinquency, The (Hirschi), 43
Center on Budget and Policy Priorities, 43
Centers for Disease Control and Prevention, 44-45
Chicago, Illinois, 25, 26, 40, 70, 71, 76-77, 81
Child abuse, 29, 37, 50-57, 90
Child development, 29
Child psychology, 34
Child Savers, 75-76
Code of Hammurabi, 27
"Code of the streets," 41-43
Coie, John D., 90
Columbine High School massacre, 13-23, 25, 40, 60, 68, 87, 89, 91
Community corrections programs, 80-85, 90
Community service, 17
Conflict resolution, 71
Contra Costa County, 37-38
Conyers, Georgia, 69
Copycat killers, 69

Counseling, 56, 57, 71, 82, 84
Crack cocaine, 44
Cruelty to animals, 88

Depression, 40, 61, 64, 68, 69
Detention centers, 83-84
Detroit, Michigan, 40
DiIulio, John J., 40, 43, 90
Discipline, 28-33, 50
Donner, Frank, 63
Doom (video game), 17, 47
Drug gangs, 44
Drug use, 43-44, 54, 66, 69
Duke University, 90
Dwyer, Kevin, 89

Earle, John, 30
Education, 29, 30
Ego, the, 35
Émile (Rousseau), 32
English law, 27, 77
Eron, Leonard, 47
Ewing, Charles Patrick, 55, 56

Federal Bureau of Investigation (FBI), 69
Films, violence in, 46, 61, 63, 66, 88
Franks, Bobby, 26
Freud, Sigmund, 35
Frontier Junior High School, 61

Index

Gardner, Neil, 19-20
Golden, Andrew, 64-67
Greene, Ronnie, Jr., 73
Group counseling, 56, 83
Group homes, 83
Grover Cleveland Elementary School, 60
Guns, 18, 19-23, 44-46, 56, 60, 61, 62, 63, 65-66, 68
Gun shows, 18
Gurian, Michael, 70

Halfway houses, 83, 84
Hall, Granville Stanley, 34
Hammurabi, 27
Harris, Eric, 13-23, 25, 35, 45, 47, 68, 69, 88
Harris, Wayne, 15-16, 18
Harvard Preparatory School, 25
Head Start, 90
Heath High School, 63
Heide, Kathleen, 55
Henry IV (king of France), 29
Heredity, 38
Hirschi, Travis, 43
Hitler, Adolf, 17
Hochhalter, Anne Marie, 19
Holstlaw, Mark, 69
House of Refuge, 75
Houston, Texas, 40
Huckabee, Mike, 66
Hull House, 76
Hypervigilance, 51-52

Id, the, 35
Illinois, 79
Inner cities, 40-43, 44, 71, 75-77
Institute of Juvenile Research, 38
Institute on Violence and Destructive Behavior, 69

Jahnke, Deborah, 54
Jahnke, Richard, 54-55
Jahnke, Richard, Jr., 54-55
Jefferson County sheriff's department, 16, 19
Johnson, Mitchell, 64-67
Jonesboro, Arkansas, 60, 64-67, 70
Justice Department, U.S., 52
Juvenile delinquency, 32, 43, 73-85
Juvenile justice system, 76-85

Kaczynski, Theodore, 68
Kinkel, Kipland, 67-68, 74, 88
Kirklin, Lance, 19
Klebold, Byron, 17
Klebold, Dylan, 13-15, 16-23, 25, 35, 45, 68, 69, 88
Klebold, Susan, 16
Klebold, Thomas, 16

Lane, John, 61
Leopold, Nathan, 25-27, 59

Levinson, John, 25-26, 27
Lewis, Dorothy, 39, 50
Littleton, Colorado, 13, 16, 23, 45, 60
Locke, John, 28
Loeb, Richard, 25-27, 59
London, England, 32
Los Angeles, California, 40
Louis XIII (king of France), 29
Louisiana, 45
Loukaitis, Barry, 61

Manes, Mark, 18
Massachusetts, 54, 57, 84
Media, violence depicted in, 17, 46-47, 61, 63, 66
Mental illness, 37-38, 64, 68
Merton, Robert, 43
Metal detectors, 71
Michigan, 71, 74
Middle Ages, 27-28
Miller, Melissa, 19
Moore, Hannah, 31
Mortal Kombat (video game), 66
Moses Lake, Washington, 60, 61, 62

National Association of School Psychologists, 89
National Center for Education Statistics, 60
National Television Violence study, 46-47

Index

Natural Born Killers (film), 61

Nazism, 17

Neglect, 53, 54

Nelme, Samuel, 49

Newcastle-upon-Tyne, Scotland, 51

New England, 30

New Haven, Connecticut, 40

New York City, 40, 71, 75

New York Times/CBS News poll, 60

Nielson, Patti, 20

Oakland, California, 37

Odessa, Texas, 70-71

Oklahoma, 45

Paducah, Kentucky, 60, 63-64, 70

Parens patriae doctrine, 77-79

Parricide, 50, 54-56

Pearl, Mississippi, 60, 62, 63, 70

Pearl High School, 62

Peer mediation, 71

Permian High School, 70-71

Philadelphia, Pennsylvania, 39, 75

Plattsburgh, New York, 16

Pomeroy, Jesse, 33, 34, 35

Pontiac, Michigan, 73

Princeton University, 40

Probation, 81-83, 84

Progressives, 76

Prothrow-Stith, Deborah, 54, 57

Prozac, 68

Psychology, 29, 34-35, 47, 64, 68, 71, 84, 89

Puritans, the, 29-30

Quake (video game), 17

Rape, 46, 61

Rap music, 47, 66, 88

Recidivism, 84

Reform schools, 76, 82

Rohrbaugh, Daniel, 19

Rousseau, Jean-Jacques, 32-33

Rural areas, 45, 59, 65

St. Louis, Missouri, 40

Sanders, Dave, 20

San Diego, California, 60

San Francisco, California, 46

Schaumburg High School, 71

Schneider, Marie, 34, 35

Scott, Rachel, 19

Self-esteem, 43, 54, 57, 68

Sexual abuse, 54

Semiautomatic weapons, 18, 45, 63

Social workers, 80

Society for the Prevention of Pauperism, 75

Spencer, Brenda, 60

Sprague, Jeff, 69-70

Springfield, Oregon, 67-68

Stiffman, Arlene, 40

Strong, Ben, 63

Suchar, Mike, 60

Suicide, 54

Superego, the, 35

Supreme Court, U.S., 74

SWAT teams, 20, 23, 71

Television, violence on, 46-47, 66, 88

Texas, 45

Thurston High School, 67-68

Tolan, Patrick, 38, 53, 90

Training schools, 83-84

Trench Coat Mafia, 16

Tutoring, 82, 83

Unabomber, 68

University of Chicago, 25

University of Michigan, 25, 47

University of Oregon, 69

University of Pennsylvania, 41

Video games, violence depicted in, 17, 47, 61, 66, 88

Violence as depicted in the media, 17, 46-47, 61, 63, 66

Index

Washington University, 40
Welfare reform, 43
West Paducah, Kentucky, 63-64. See also Paducah, Kentucky
Westside Middle School, 65, 67

When Children Kill (Ewing), 55
Why Kids Kill Parents (Heide), 55
Wilson, Ralph, Jr., 66-67
Wisener, Donna Marie, 50
Woodham, Luke, 62, 63

Wragg, Burton, 60
Wright, Sharon, 65

Zero tolerance policy, 70

Picture Credits

page

2:	©Reuters/Rick Wilking/ Archive Photos		Archive Photos	64:	©Reuters/John Sommers II/ Archive Photos
12:	AP/Wide World Photos	34:	Corbis		
14:	©Reuters/Ho/ Archive Photos	36:	AP/Wide World Photos	67:	©Reuters/Ho/ Archive Photos
		41:	Photo Researchers, Inc.		
15:	©Reuters/Ho/ Archive Photos	42:	©Reuters/Jeff Mitchell/ Archive Photos	70:	AP/Wide World Photos
21:	©Reuters/Gary Caskey/Archive Photos	45:	AP/Wide World Photos	72:	AP/Wide World Photos
		48:	©Corel Corporation	77:	Corbis
22:	©Reuters/Jeff Mitchell/ Archive Photos	51:	©Popperfoto/ Archive Photos	78:	The Library of Congress #LC-UCSZ62-48574
24:	Corbis	52:	Hannah Gal/Corbis	81:	Corbis
28:	Corbis	56:	AP/Wide World Photos	83:	©Corel Corporation
31:	Corbis	58-59:	©Reuters/Paul Carte- Register/Archive Photos	86-87:	AP/Wide World Photos
32:	©Popperfoto/			89:	©Corel Corporation
		62:	AP/Wide World Photos		

RICHARD WORTH has 30 years of experience as a writer, trainer, and video producer. He has written more than 25 books, including *The Four Levers of Corporate Change*, a best-selling business book. Many of his books are for young adults, on topics that include family living, foreign affairs, biography, and history. He has also written an eight-part radio series on New York mayor Fiorello LaGuardia, which aired on National Public Radio. He presents writing and public speaking seminars for corporate executives.

AUSTIN SARAT is William Nelson Cromwell Professor of Jurisprudence and Political Science at Amherst College, where he also chairs the Department of Law, Jurisprudence and Social Thought. Professor Sarat is the author or editor of 23 books and numerous scholarly articles. Among his books are *Law's Violence, Sitting in Judgment: Sentencing the White Collar Criminal,* and *Justice and Injustice in Law and Legal Theory.* He has received many academic awards and held several prestigious fellowships. In addition, he is a nationally recognized teacher and educator whose teaching has been featured in the *New York Times*, on the *Today* show, and on National Public Radio's *Fresh Air.*

25 UPPER JAY ROAD
UPPER JAY, NY 11112-268

ST. JOSEPH'S COLLEGE CALLAHAN LIBRARY

3 1 0 01473 854

Callahan LIBRARY
ST. JOSEPH'S COLLEGE
25 Audubon Avenue
Patchogue, NY 11772-2800

2003 VOR Cr 5 12
CH
Worth, Richard
Children, Violence, and
Murder

J